INDUSTRIALIZE

The Insider's Guide

to

Industrial Real Estate

Chad Griffiths

ISBN: 978-1-0689474-1-4
First Edition, 2025

Acknowledgements

My passion for industrial real estate has been fuelled by countless people who each played a part in this book.

Lord Alfred Tennyson put it best:

"I am a part of all that I've met".

Some directly contributed, others indirectly (or even unknowingly) also had a big role.

A big thank you to the following:

Ryan Brown, Darcie Brown, Vincenzo Caputo, Drew Joslin, Kevin Mockford, Kim Sarnecki, Chad Snow, Bo Baron, Jeff Beals, Brian Burke, Darin Brindle, Matt Carroll, Tyler Cauble, John Croft, Sean Dalfen, Coy Davidson, Nick Eyhorn, Michael Golden, Aaron Halfacre, Zach Harris, Wyatt Hammond, Shane Henke, Todd Hirsch, Douglas Kiersey, Bob Knakal, Ryan Koehn, Mark Lee Levine, Bryon Leece, Peter Linneman, Mike Lipsey, Mike Mack, Jeremy Mercer, Kristen McTiernan, Jay Olshonsky, Adrian Ponsen, Chris Powers, Matthew Rand, Ronald Rohde, Walt Rakowich, Skylar Romines, Kevin Runion, Rod Santomassimo, Sandy Shindleman, Robert Thornburgh, Jim Tomkins, Percy Woods, SIOR Global, NAIOP, members of the Industrial Insider's group, and each and every person I've been fortunate to interview on my podcast.

And of course, my family who has been very understanding every time I wanted to detour to an industrial park while on vacation.

I cannot thank you all enough.

Foreword

By **Tyler Cauble**

I met Chad Griffiths back in 2017 when he featured my Instagram account in a Forbes article he was writing on the top commercial real estate accounts to follow. At the time, I was curious—what else was this broker doing to market himself so well that Forbes came calling? That single article led to a conversation, which turned into a friendship, and over the years I've watched Chad continue to show up, over and over again, with consistency, generosity, and real insight into the world of industrial real estate.

If there's one word that defines Chad, it's *commitment*. For over a decade now, he's been creating content, analyzing the industrial market, and helping brokers, investors, and developers understand the nuances of this asset class. He's not just someone who works in the business—he's someone who's helped shape the conversation around it. From his blog to his podcast appearances (including joining me as co-host on *The Commercial Real Estate Investor Podcast's* Brokers Round Table), Chad has become one of the most trusted voices in industrial real estate.

That's why *Industrialize* is such an important book. What Chad has pulled together here is the most in-depth, tactical, and thorough guide to industrial real estate I've ever seen. It's not a surface-level overview or a glorified sales pitch. It's a deep dive—down to individual chapters on sprinklers, column grids, ceiling heights, and site layouts. He covers everything from manufacturing and warehousing to land development, zoning, and financing. If you've ever wanted a single resource that could take you from "I don't really know how industrial works" to "I'm ready to confidently take action," this is it.

Whether you're a broker trying to better serve your clients, an investor building your portfolio, or a developer eyeing your next project, you will walk away from this book with a deeper understanding of how industrial real estate functions—and how to identify real opportunities within it.

Industrial has been the hot topic in commercial real estate for the better part of a decade, driven by the rise of e-commerce and only accelerated by the pandemic. While some markets may be stabilizing today, there's no doubt in my mind that this asset class will continue to grow and evolve in response to consumer and business demand. It's not going away. If anything, it's becoming more essential.

I consider myself a generalist in the commercial real estate world—I've worked across asset types for years—but even as someone who started doing industrial deals in 2013 and now owns over 1.5 million square feet of industrial space across self-storage, flex, distribution, and manufacturing, I still found insights in this book that leveled up my understanding.

It's also been a joy to watch Chad grow as a YouTuber, sharing his expertise with the world and building a community of people who genuinely learn from him. *Industrialize* is the next logical step in that journey—and I can't wait to see where it takes him, and you, next.

Let's get into it.

Preface

This book provides a comprehensive overview of industrial real estate, covering foundational principles, advanced strategies, and practical insights critical for success in this dynamic sector. You'll explore the core aspects of industrial properties, including manufacturing facilities, warehouses, distribution centers, flex spaces, and specialized industrial buildings. Each chapter delivers clear explanations, real-world examples, and actionable advice that will help you understand how industrial real estate functions and how to navigate its unique challenges and opportunities.

Whether you're a seasoned professional aiming to deepen your expertise, an investor looking for opportunities in an often-overlooked asset class, or someone new to the industry seeking a solid introduction, this book is tailored to your needs. It distills complex market dynamics, tenant considerations, property evaluations, construction processes, and investment strategies into accessible, practical guidance.

My credentials for writing this book are built upon two decades of direct experience in the industrial real estate sector. Since entering the field in 2005, I've navigated countless transactions as a broker, investor, and advisor. Additionally, my insights have been enriched through extensive conversations with top industry leaders and experts featured on my podcast, providing a wide-ranging perspective on best practices and emerging trends. I've had the honor of conducting over 150 interviews and the insights gained during these discussions are found throughout the chapters.

By reading this book, you'll gain valuable knowledge that will enable you to confidently engage with all facets of industrial real estate. Ultimately, your success in this industry will rest on mastering three key fundamentals:

Understand the tenant, understand the building, understand the market.

I hope you find this book as beneficial and rewarding to read as it was for me to write.

Chad Griffiths

Table of Contents

1

What Is Industrial Real Estate?

INDUSTRIAL REAL ESTATE is everywhere. In North America alone, industrial real estate is a $2 trillion market that impacts every part of daily life—from the food we eat to the packages delivered to our doors.

The concept of constructing spaces dedicated to industry isn't new. Centuries ago, simple structures were built to store goods or produce essential items. Today, industrial real estate has evolved dramatically, becoming the backbone of global commerce and everyday life.

Industrial real estate includes properties specifically designed to support essential business operations—so integral that modern life would be unimaginable without them. From manufacturing and storage to high-tech data centers, industrial real estate quietly powers the modern world.

The 2020 pandemic underscored the critical role of industrial real estate. While offices and retail spaces temporarily shut down, warehouses and factories remained operational, ensuring essentials like food, medical supplies, and online orders continued flowing. Industrial real estate doesn't just support businesses—it supports society.

Industrial real estate is divided into distinct categories, which we'll explore further in upcoming chapters:

Factories

Facilities specifically designed for manufacturing, processing, or assembling goods from raw or semi-finished materials.

Warehouses

Buildings primarily used for storage, distribution, logistics management, and freight handling.

Flex Properties

Industrial-zoned properties combining industrial space with other uses such as offices, labs, showrooms, or mixed-use business spaces. Common examples include research facilities, self-storage, and hybrid spaces.

Industrial Outdoor Storage (IOS)

These properties offer secure outdoor storage for equipment, vehicles, or materials and typically feature large yard spaces with minimal structures.

TechFlex

High-tech industrial facilities like data centers, semiconductor fabrication plants (fabs), electric vehicle manufacturing plants, and other specialized, technology-intensive spaces.

Historical Perspective

Industrial real estate has a rich history, evolving from basic storage sheds and workshops into the sophisticated, purpose-built facilities seen today. Its growth has closely paralleled advancements in technology, transportation, and global trade, becoming a cornerstone of economic development.

Economic Impact

The industrial real estate sector drives significant economic activity, creating millions of jobs across construction, manufacturing, logistics, and supply chain management. It stimulates regional growth by attracting businesses and encouraging infrastructure development.

Without this infrastructure, global trade would face significant disruptions.

Warehouses and distribution centers strategically located near ports, railways, and highways ensure seamless movement of goods worldwide.

Modern Trends

Industrial real estate continually evolves. E-commerce has dramatically increased demand for warehousing and fulfillment centers. "Companies are increasingly investing in automation, robotics, and energy-efficient facilities to meet evolving industry demands.

Future Outlook

The future of industrial real estate is promising. Urban logistics, multi-story warehouses, manufacturing resurgence, and smart technologies will further redefine the sector. The demand for innovative, adaptable spaces will grow as businesses evolve and consumer expectations shift.

Two Key Themes Keep these two fundamental concepts in mind as we explore industrial real estate throughout this book:

1. Tenant-Centric Value: the primary purpose of industrial properties is to support the businesses that occupy them. The usability, functionality, and value of any industrial property ultimately depend on how effectively it serves tenants. Simply put, a property's worth directly ties to the rent a company is willing to pay for its use.

2. Risk Management First: Always understand and quantify downside risks first. While developing forecasts and proformas can be engaging, the primary focus must remain on objectively identifying and managing potential risks.

These guiding principles will serve as a compass for navigating the complexities and opportunities of industrial real estate.

2

Factories & Manufacturing Facilities

MANUFACTURING FACILITIES OPERATE on a deceptively simple premise: raw materials arrive, undergo transformation through manufacturing, production, or assembly, and leave as finished products. Yet beneath this straightforward process is immense complexity, shaped by diverse operational needs and specific facility requirements.

Types of Manufacturing Facilities

When most people think of manufacturing, they might imagine heavy industrial facilities, such as large factories or even old, dirty buildings. However, Manufacturing spans a broad spectrum, from heavy industrial properties to lighter manufacturing spaces.

Let's break it down into sub-categories:

Heavy Industrial

A metal fabricator that welds, cuts, burns, and machines raw materials exemplify this category. Significant noise, heavy equipment, and emissions are common characteristics.

Figure 1: A Heavy Industrial Building

Medium Industrial

A plastic injection molding manufacturer is an example of medium industrial. Operations typically involve moderate power requirements, specialized equipment (like injection molding machines), and moderate yard space for storage.

Light Industrial

Companies assembling computer parts or electronics often operate in clean, quiet facilities resembling office spaces rather than traditional factories.

Figure 2: Computer fabrication inside a light industrial building

Given the diverse types of businesses, assigning labels to properties can be challenging. Sometimes it's helpful to consider zoning classifications.

Zoning Considerations

Zoning regulations determine which businesses can operate within a property. Municipalities often classify industrial zoning into subcategories (light, medium, or heavy industrial), though some apply broader, or even narrower, definitions.

Key point: Always verify zoning to ensure the intended use is permitted before committing to a property. Unless working in a rare area without zoning laws, confirm that prospective tenants can secure the necessary municipal permits. Contracts should include conditions ensuring tenants obtain necessary permits before proceeding.

Customization for Tenants

Manufacturing properties must meet tenants' specific operational needs. Ensuring facilities remain competitive within their class involves addressing several critical considerations:

Electrical Power

Adequate electrical capacity is crucial for manufacturing operations reliant on heavy machinery and specialized equipment. Companies running heavy machinery, robotics, welding equipment, or other high-powered industrial processes typically require substantial electrical capacity (commonly 480-volt, three-phase service). Property owners must confirm existing capabilities and clearly document them, including transformer capacity and panel configurations. Evaluating upgrade costs early can help landlords attract tenants reliant on power-intensive equipment. Prospective tenants should always perform detailed electrical audits and verify infrastructure independently to ensure compatibility and to avoid costly surprises after occupancy.

Cranes and Specialized Equipment

Many manufacturers require overhead cranes for efficient and safe material handling, assembly, or heavy fabrication processes. Facilities designed to accommodate cranes from the outset offer significant competitive advantages. These properties include crane rails, suitable column spacing, adequate ceiling heights, and structural supports engineered specifically for overhead lifting. Conversely, retrofitting an existing building to install cranes later often incurs substantial costs due to necessary structural reinforcements, extensive recertification processes, and potential production disruptions during modifications.

Building Ratios and Interior Configurations

The ratio of office space to production or warehouse areas can significantly influence a property's attractiveness. Facilities that deviate substantially from market norms may necessitate expensive reconfiguration to meet tenant requirements. Examples include properties with excessive or insufficient office space relative to warehouse or production space. Modular interior walls, flexible office layouts, and adaptable production spaces are advantageous in accommodating various tenant needs without extensive renovations.

Structural Integrity and Load Capacities

Manufacturing companies utilizing heavy machinery, large-scale assembly equipment, or dense materials storage must ensure the facility's structural integrity aligns with their operational demands. Key structural considerations include verifying concrete slab thickness and reinforcement, mezzanine load capacities, floor flatness for equipment stability, and column spacing to accommodate machinery layouts. Tenants often conduct detailed structural assessments during due diligence to confirm that existing specifications align with operational requirements.

Site Layout and Yard Space

The site coverage ratio (building footprint relative to site size) is crucial for manufacturing properties. Adequate yard space is essential for storing equipment, raw materials, finished goods, and vehicle maneuverability. Specific site considerations include:

> **Gravel Quality**: High-quality, compacted gravel is important to ensure proper drainage, avoid soft areas, and accommodate heavy vehicles and equipment without damage.
>
> **Exterior Lighting and Security**: Robust outdoor lighting and secure perimeter fencing provide essential security, enhance operational safety, and ensure regulatory compliance.
>
> **Truck and Equipment Maneuverability**: Sufficient turning radii, paved access points, and clearly marked staging areas enhance logistical efficiency and reduce bottlenecks.

Fire Safety, Air Quality, and Environmental Considerations

> **Sprinkler Systems**: Sprinkler systems are typically mandatory for fire safety in manufacturing environments due to high risks associated with machinery, storage, and combustible materials. Understanding whether sprinkler installations are driven by municipal codes, insurance requirements, or tenant operational standards is critical, as installation or upgrades can be costly.
>
> **Makeup Air Units** (MAUs): MAUs are essential for maintaining indoor air quality by replenishing fresh outdoor air in spaces with significant exhaust or particulate generation. While not universally mandatory, they are increasingly required by municipalities and highly desirable for tenants to meet workplace safety and comfort standards.
>
> **Environmental Compliance**: Manufacturing properties must comply with local environmental regulations, particularly concerning waste management, emissions, noise, and chemical storage. Facilities proactively equipped with containment, filtration, or specialized waste systems have a competitive edge.

Adaptability and Futureproofing:

To remain competitive, industrial properties should incorporate flexible designs that accommodate diverse processes and future tenant needs.

Examples include reinforced floor slabs for heavy machinery, expandable electrical capacity, modular office layouts, and infrastructure capable of supporting future automation or technological upgrades.

Expert Insight

"When you're buying manufacturing real estate, you're knowingly accepting a binary risk—either the tenant stays or they don't. That's why it's crucial to buy properties where the tenant is producing something essential, durable, and embedded into the backbone of the economy. You need assets that have survived globalization, outsourcing trends, and economic cycles, because that's what creates long-term stability."
—Aaron Halfacre, CEO of Modiv Industrial

Manufacturing facilities embody much more than physical structures—they are intricate systems critical to our economy. Halfacre's observation underscores the importance of understanding the long-term sustainability of the products being manufactured, along with tenant stability. Selecting facilities aligned with core economic functions, with tenants who have endured various market disruptions, significantly reduces investment risk and secures long-term value.

Summary

Manufacturing facilities are inherently diverse, reflecting the unique operational demands of their occupants. While no property can meet every company's needs, designing flexible, adaptable facilities that address tenant-specific requirements ensures long-term competitiveness. Properties addressing power availability, structural integrity, yard functionality, safety systems, and environmental compliance will attract tenants more effectively, maximize occupancy, and secure long-term property value.

3

Warehouses / Distribution

Centers

WAREHOUSING INVOLVES THE CRITICAL process of efficiently managing the flow of goods— receiving products, storing, sorting or repackaging them, and shipping them out again. Achieving this requires warehouses to have strategic design features, such as accessible roadways, optimized loading areas, adequate ceiling heights, and flexible column grids.

The Role of Warehousing

Fundamentally, a warehouse serves to store products. Raw materials and semi-finished goods stay stored until production requires them, while finished products await shipment or sale. Warehouses often support additional activities, such as unpackaging, sorting, and repackaging. For instance, break bulk operators receive large shipments, divide them into smaller batches, and redistribute them to various destinations.

Sub-Categories of Warehousing

Warehousing includes several specialized categories tailored to unique operational needs:

Big Box Warehouses

Facilities typically over 100,000 sq. ft., strategically located near major transportation hubs to efficiently handle large volumes of inventory. These warehouses are ideal for large-scale logistics operations and major retailers needing significant storage capacity and rapid throughput.

Figure 3: A Big Box Warehouse

Distribution Centers

Facilities optimized for rapid turnover of goods, essential for maintaining smooth supply chain operations. These centers are strategically located near transportation hubs to minimize transit times and lower logistics costs.

Fulfillment Centers

Designed specifically for processing and shipping individual online orders, often leveraging advanced automation. Efficiency in order picking and packaging is crucial, as delays can directly impact customer satisfaction and brand reputation.

Cross Docking Facilities

Warehouses designed specifically for the rapid transfer of goods from inbound to outbound transportation, minimizing storage time. Effective cross docking reduces inventory holding costs and accelerates the distribution process, making it ideal for perishable goods or fast-moving consumer products. These facilities typically feature multiple loading docks arranged to streamline the movement of goods directly between trucks or containers, significantly enhancing supply chain efficiency and responsiveness.

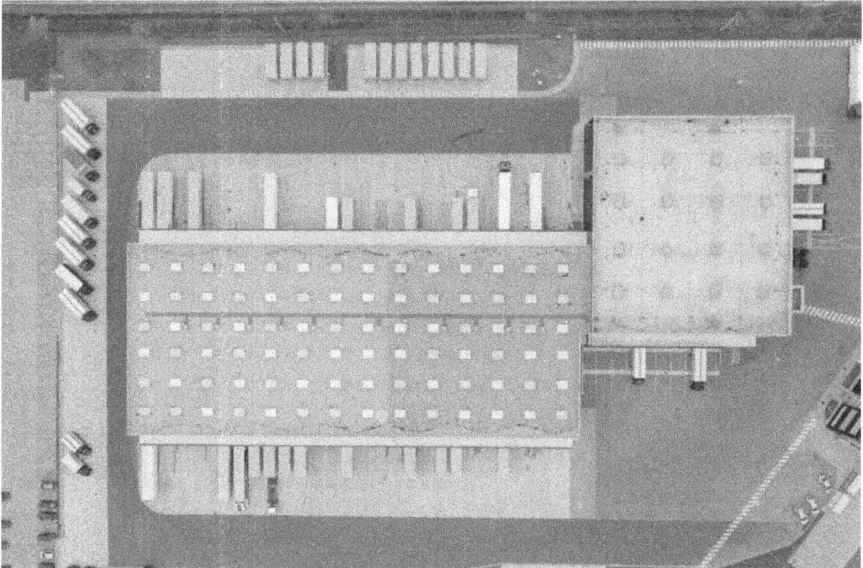

Figure 4: A cross dock facility

High Bay Industrial

Facilities designed with very high ceilings, typically over 30 feet, to accommodate vertical storage solutions and automated retrieval systems. These warehouses maximize cubic storage space, improving inventory management efficiency and reducing overall real estate footprint.

Cold Storage Warehouses

Facilities featuring refrigeration systems for storing temperature-sensitive products, ranging from fully refrigerated buildings to specialized rooms within larger facilities. Maintaining precise temperature control is critical, as even minor fluctuations can result in significant product loss and regulatory compliance issues.

Flex Industrial

Hybrid spaces combining warehouse functions with office or light industrial uses; discussed further in the next chapter. Their adaptability is especially beneficial to growing businesses needing flexibility to scale operations or shift usage rapidly.

Specialized Warehouses

Properties catering to unique needs, including hazardous materials, high-security storage, or international bonded storage, requiring advanced features or strict compliance measures. Due to specialized regulatory requirements, these warehouses often require significant upfront investment but can offer premium leasing rates and high occupancy levels.

Small Bay Industrial

Smaller warehouse units, often under 10,000 sq. ft., designed for small-to-medium businesses requiring storage, distribution, or light manufacturing space. These facilities typically offer more flexible leasing arrangements and cater to local or regional tenants.

Differentiating these sub-categories ultimately depends on understanding how trucks access and leave the property, as well as what activities occur within each facility. Key factors include the frequency, timing, and size of shipments, truck maneuverability, the arrangement and quantity of loading docks, and proximity to transportation routes. Internally, differentiation considers storage duration, handling complexity, product sensitivity, and the extent of automation or specialized infrastructure required. Clear distinctions in these operational dynamics are critical for ensuring optimal functionality, efficiency, and alignment with specific tenant needs and supply chain demands. However, it's important to recognize that significant overlap can exist between these categories, and in practical terms, overly technical distinctions may not always be necessary or beneficial, especially when a facility serves multiple purposes or evolves over time.

Key Physical Attributes for Warehouses

To meet tenant expectations, warehouse facilities must prioritize several critical features:

Road Access and Truck Maneuverability

Efficient access from highways and ample space for semi-truck navigation and loading/unloading are critical. Limited access or poor maneuverability can hinder operational efficiency and reduce tenant satisfaction.

Ceiling Heights

Modern warehouse tenants typically seek clear ceiling heights of at least 28 feet, with newer buildings commonly exceeding 34 feet. Lower ceilings may require retrofitting or lower lease rates, though some operations, like roofing companies, can thrive in lower-ceiling spaces.

Column Grid

Column spacing typically ranges from 40 to 55 feet. Wider spacing offers greater flexibility but may increase construction costs. Assess column grid spacing based on the specific operational needs of prospective tenants.

Roofs, Structure, and Maintenance

During due diligence, evaluate roof conditions, foundation integrity, and site paving. Sophisticated tenants often push these costs to landlords, making them unrecoverable via operating expenses. Key areas include roof repairs, asphalt or concrete maintenance, and foundation inspections.

Sprinkler Systems

Sprinklers are frequently mandated by tenants, insurers, or municipalities. Common types include Early Suppression, Fast Response (ESFR) systems and in-rack systems, which require regular inspection and certification. Installation or upgrades can be costly.

Air Quality and Ventilation

Makeup air systems, replacing indoor air with outdoor air, are increasingly requested or even mandated by municipalities, especially for operations using propane forklifts or other machinery. These systems often entail significant installation costs.

Super-flat Floors

Increasingly important for tenants using advanced robotics or precision material handling equipment, super-flat floors facilitate optimal operation. This trend will likely continue as automation grows.

Lighting

Modern lighting, such as LED or T8HO, significantly enhances functionality and tenant appeal. Upgrading outdated lighting systems, such as mercury halide bulbs, can be costly but significantly improves efficiency and tenant appeal.

Office Buildout

Most warehouses require 5–20% of their space to be allocated for offices. Too little or excessive office space may necessitate costly modifications. Balancing this effectively is crucial to tenant satisfaction and long-term flexibility.

Specialized Tenant Requirements

Some tenants have unique property needs, for example:

Granite Wholesalers: Require reinforced floors and overhead cranes.
Temperature-Sensitive Goods: Demand specialized refrigeration/HVAC systems and structural support.

Summary

Terminology and definitions will vary considerably. Not just between different markets but even across different companies within the same market.

One person might refer to a distribution center simply as a warehouse, while another might use fulfillment center and cross dock facility interchangeably.

This potential confusion highlights one of the underlying themes of the book: fully understand exactly what the tenant needs in a building.

Effective warehousing relies on efficiently managing the inbound and outbound flow of goods. Key warehouse features—such as optimal ceiling heights, flexible column spacing, proper lighting, and robust air systems—directly impact operational efficiency and tenant appeal. Understanding and accommodating tenant requirements further maximizes property value and market competitiveness.

4

Flex Industrial

FLEX INDUSTRIAL PROPERTIES represent a versatile category within industrial real estate—buildings zoned for industrial use but adaptable enough to accommodate non-traditional tenants. These properties bridge traditional industrial and commercial uses, offering flexibility for a diverse range of businesses, from offices and retail showrooms to specialized niche operations.

What is Flex Industrial?

At its core, flex industrial properties are designed to meet diverse needs. They maintain industrial zoning and structural characteristics yet are frequently used for purposes beyond traditional industrial applications. While spaces are typically smaller (often under 10,000 square feet), they're sometimes referred to as Small Bay Industrial or Contractor Garages due to their adaptable layouts.

A Real-World Example

Consider the building where my own office is located. Situated in an industrial park and zoned industrial, it maintains an industrial appearance but also enjoys prominent frontage on a major roadway, giving it quasi-retail exposure.

Figure 5: Example of a Flex Building

Thanks to its flexible design and location, it accommodates diverse tenants such as a flower shop, a hot tub retailer, an equestrian supply store, and a cabinet showroom. None are traditional industrial businesses, yet all thrive in this adaptable space. This flexibility is the essence of flex industrial.

Characteristics of Flex Industrial Properties

Industrial Zoning: Allows for a broader range of uses compared to commercial zoning.
Quasi-Retail Locations: Often positioned on major roads or within industrial parks, offering visibility and accessibility.
Adaptable Space: Typically feature open floor plans easily tailored for varied uses.
Diverse Tenant Mix: Occupied by businesses ranging from retail and offices to specialty services and labs.

Common Uses of Flex Industrial Properties

Office Space: Cost-effective and conveniently located office hubs.
Retail Showrooms: Ideal for furniture, cabinetry, appliances, or specialty retail due to industrial zoning and retail visibility.
Specialty Retail: Niche businesses such as flower shops, pet care facilities, or boutique stores.
Research & Laboratories: Suitable for light R&D activities due to open

layouts and flexible zoning.

Hybrid Spaces: Combining offices, retail, and light industrial activities under one roof.

The Appeal of Flex Industrial

Flex industrial's appeal lies in its adaptability to diverse needs. For property owners, this versatility translates to a broader tenant pool and higher occupancy rates. For tenants, flex spaces provide cost-effective, customizable locations tailored to their unique operational needs.

Challenges with Flex Industrial

Zoning Conflicts: Non-traditional uses may challenge industrial zoning limits, often requiring municipal approvals or rezoning.

Specialized Requirements: Businesses needing extensive parking or unique buildouts may find limitations in flex properties.

Tenant Turnover: Diverse tenant types can lead to increased turnover compared to traditional industrial or retail tenants, potentially increasing leasing and management complexity.

Examples of Flex Industrial Uses

Flex industrial properties accommodate a surprisingly wide variety of tenants. Some real-world examples include:

Recreation: Trampoline parks, go-karting, climbing gyms, soccer/baseball facilities, axe throwing, laser tag.

Entertainment & Events: Wedding venues, film studios, banquet halls, escape rooms, museums.

Retail & Specialty Shops: Furniture showrooms, thrift stores, antique stores, flower shops, farmers markets.

Health & Wellness: Fitness centers, hyperbaric oxygen spas, indoor farms, medical labs.

Educational & Creative: Music schools, robotics labs, art galleries, co-working spaces, training centers.

Unique Uses: Breweries, wineries, gun ranges, archery centers, doggy daycares, bottle depots.

If you encounter a unique use I haven't listed, snap a picture and share it with me on X @chadgriffiths.

Summary

Flex industrial properties are the chameleons of industrial real estate—adaptable, versatile, and uniquely positioned to accommodate diverse tenant requirements. Whether serving as office spaces, retail showrooms, laboratories, or hybrid operations, their flexibility offers significant advantages to both tenants and property owners. Though they come with unique challenges, the dynamic nature of flex industrial spaces makes them essential components in today's commercial real estate market.

5

Industrial Outdoor Storage (IOS)

INDUSTRIAL OUTDOOR STORAGE (IOS) describes industrial-zoned properties primarily featuring extensive outdoor spaces designed specifically to store equipment, vehicles, materials, or containers. These properties have become crucial assets within sectors like construction, logistics, manufacturing, and transportation, particularly as demand for efficient, cost-effective storage has surged. Although the concept has existed for over a century, the term "Industrial Outdoor Storage" recently gained prominence, drawing attention from investors and businesses alike.

The Basics of IOS

IOS properties typically have a low site coverage ratio, meaning buildings occupy less than 20% of the total land area. Some IOS sites consist purely of open yard space, while others include complementary structures like small warehouses, workshops, or office trailers. These additional structures significantly enhance the property's versatility and tenant appeal by providing spaces for maintenance, repairs, and administrative tasks.

A Real-World Perspective

Jeremy Mercer, President of Matador Capital, highlights the importance of integrating functional structures alongside open storage areas. Mercer notes that IOS properties featuring shops or other complementary buildings typically experience faster lease-up and greater market appeal. Conversely, properties consisting solely of open land (e.g., truck yards or container storage yards) often face longer leasing periods due to limited functionality and narrower tenant attraction.

The Evolution of Industrial Outdoor Storage

The practice of using outdoor land for industrial storage dates back to the late 19th and early 20th centuries, coinciding with rapid urban expansion and industrial growth. Initially informal, outdoor storage gradually evolved into a formally recognized land-use category through advances in urban planning and zoning regulations. The modern term "Industrial Outdoor Storage" emerged to clearly differentiate these specialized outdoor storage facilities from traditional indoor warehouses, emphasizing their strategic placement near transportation corridors, logistical hubs, and industrial districts.

Modern Trends and Demand Drivers

Several key factors drive the increased demand for IOS:

E-commerce Growth: The rapid increase in online shopping and direct-to-consumer deliveries has amplified the demand for logistics hubs to store vehicles, shipping containers, trailers, and related equipment.

Construction and Infrastructure Expansion: Rising investment in infrastructure, residential, and commercial developments requires substantial outdoor storage capacity for construction materials, heavy equipment, and machinery.

Supply Chain Resilience: Recent global disruptions have underscored the need for accessible and flexible storage solutions for oversized goods, spare equipment, and inventory overflow.

Urbanization and Land Scarcity: With limited land available in urban cores, IOS properties located near urban and suburban areas provide invaluable storage solutions for businesses seeking proximity to customers and infrastructure.

Despite generally lower lease rates compared to indoor warehousing, IOS properties remain highly profitable due to lower construction and ongoing maintenance costs and their inherent flexibility in accommodating diverse storage needs.

Key Features of IOS Properties

Strategic Location: Optimally located near major highways, intermodal terminals, ports, airports, or industrial and commercial hubs to facilitate quick transport and operational efficiency.

Security and Accessibility: Typically include basic security measures such as perimeter fencing, controlled access gates, lighting, and sometimes surveillance systems. While security tends to be simpler than indoor facilities, secure and accessible properties command higher market interest.

Surface Material and Durability: Surfaces are commonly gravel, crushed stone, asphalt, or reinforced concrete, specifically designed to support heavy industrial loads, vehicle movement, and withstand prolonged exposure to weather.

Utility Infrastructure: Utility availability varies widely; some IOS sites provide basic utilities such as electricity, lighting, water, drainage, and sometimes minimal office facilities or sanitation infrastructure.

Challenges and Opportunities

Tenant Pool Limitations: Properties without structural enhancements or limited utilities typically appeal to a narrower segment of potential tenants, often requiring owners to invest further in infrastructure to broaden appeal.

Zoning and Regulatory Complexity: Navigating local zoning laws, permitting processes, and environmental regulations can significantly impact the development and usability of IOS sites. Restrictions on specific uses or environmental remediation requirements may delay projects or limit operational flexibility.

Tenant-Specific Infrastructure Needs: Certain industries have specialized requirements, such as reinforced surfaces for heavy machinery, maintenance workshops, electrical infrastructure, or environmental containment measures. Addressing these specialized needs can significantly enhance marketability but increase upfront costs.

Investment Considerations

From an investor's perspective, IOS properties often provide attractive yields, reduced capital investment, and operational simplicity relative to traditional industrial real estate. However, thorough due diligence is crucial, focusing on zoning compliance, environmental assessments, market demand analysis, and infrastructure evaluation.

An Insider's Perspective

Justin Horowitz, Principal at Cooper Horowitz, highlights the unique strategic advantage of IOS properties:

"These sites are mission-critical to tenants in desired locations. If the zoning and

environmental aspects check out, and you understand the leasing market, you're sitting on gold. Nobody's building this in cities anymore—making well-zoned IOS properties incredibly valuable."

Horowitz's insights stress the complexity and essential due diligence needed for IOS investments. While zoning challenges, environmental considerations, and limited development opportunities present barriers, they also create a significant competitive advantage for investors who thoroughly understand and address these factors.

Summary

Industrial Outdoor Storage has evolved into a critical asset class within the industrial real estate sector, supporting pivotal industries ranging from logistics and e-commerce to construction and heavy manufacturing. The most successful IOS properties integrate extensive outdoor space with strategically developed facilities and infrastructure, balancing flexibility with specific tenant needs to optimize profitability, tenant retention, and long-term asset value.

6

TechFlex / Powered Industrial

TECHFLEX, ALSO KNOWN AS Powered Industrial, represents a cutting-edge category of industrial real estate engineered specifically for high-tech industries. These facilities are designed to meet significant demands for power, water, infrastructure reliability, and network connectivity, making them essential for data centers, gigafactories, semiconductor fabs, and electric vehicle (EV) manufacturing plants.

Defining Characteristics of TechFlex Properties

Massive Power Requirements:

TechFlex properties have extraordinary power needs far surpassing typical industrial facilities.

For perspective, a standard large industrial building may access around 2,000 amps (approximately 1 megawatt, MW).

In contrast, even a smaller data center typically requires at least 20 MW (around 40,000 amps). Securing this substantial power capacity often presents the greatest challenge in site selection.

Water Demand:

Many TechFlex properties, especially semiconductor fabs and gigafactories, require significant water resources for cooling and manufacturing processes. Proximity to reliable water sources and advanced water management systems are critical.

Backup Systems:

To ensure uninterrupted operations, TechFlex properties frequently include substantial backup generators and redundant infrastructure. This is especially crucial for data centers, where even brief downtime can cause significant financial and operational disruptions.

Resilient Locations:

TechFlex facilities are strategically located in areas with minimal environmental risks, such as earthquakes or extreme weather, ensuring operational stability and continuity.

Network Connectivity:

High-speed, robust internet connectivity is vital. Facilities like data centers and semiconductor fabs require proximity to fiber optic networks or major data exchanges, ensuring low latency, high bandwidth, and redundancy. Multiple connectivity pathways are often established to mitigate single points of failure.

Key Industries and Uses

Semiconductor Fabs (Fabrication Plants):

Semiconductor manufacturing facilities require ultra-clean environments, precise temperature control, massive amounts of power, and reliable water supply. Additionally, proximity to skilled labor and supply chain hubs is crucial.

Gigafactories:

Gigafactories produce lithium-ion batteries at scale, primarily for EVs and energy storage systems. They require significant electricity and water resources and are frequently located near renewable energy sources to manage costs and sustainability goals.

EV Manufacturing:

Electric vehicle plants combine traditional manufacturing processes with extensive power demands and battery storage capabilities, often located alongside gigafactories to streamline production efficiency.

Figure 6: An EV manufacturing facility

Data Centers:

Data centers form the backbone of today's digital economy, housing critical IT infrastructure necessary for storing, processing, and distributing vast amounts of data around the globe. Driven by exponential growth in cloud computing, artificial intelligence, streaming media, and online transactions, the need for data centers has dramatically increased. However, developing these highly specialized industrial facilities is far from straightforward and presents unique complexities and challenges.

Complexity and Design

At their core, data centers are highly specialized industrial properties requiring detailed planning and sophisticated engineering. Each facility must accommodate sensitive electronic equipment, extensive networking infrastructure, and critical data storage systems. Because reliability and redundancy are essential, data centers typically integrate advanced electrical and mechanical systems rarely seen in other types of industrial facilities.

These include:

Uninterrupted Power Supply: Backup power systems that instantly activate during outages, ensuring continuous operation.

Redundant Cooling Systems: Sophisticated HVAC and chilled-water cooling technologies to manage enormous heat outputs from densely packed servers.

Fire Suppression and Security Systems: State-of-the-art fire protection (often using non-water-based suppression methods) and stringent security protocols designed to safeguard sensitive data and equipment.

Advanced Networking Infrastructure: High-speed, redundant fiber optic networks connecting data centers directly to major telecommunications hubs, ensuring rapid data transfer and minimal latency.

Given these complexities, data center projects require collaboration among specialized architects, engineers, contractors, power providers, network experts, and security specialists. The integration and coordination of these disparate disciplines contribute to a uniquely challenging development process.

Development Timelines

The development timeline for a data center can far exceed traditional industrial buildings, often spanning two to four years from initial conception to operational readiness. Some hyperscale facilities—massive data centers typically operated by large technology companies—can take even longer, particularly when accounting for the intricate design phase, infrastructure coordination, and extensive equipment procurement processes.

Key phases of the timeline typically include:

Site Selection and Due Diligence (3–6 months): Intensive evaluations to determine proximity to fiber optic networks, ample power sources, reliable utility providers, suitable geography, risk profiles, and political or regulatory environments.

Design and Planning Phase (6–12 months): Detailed engineering designs addressing infrastructure redundancies, layout efficiency, electrical load capacities, cooling system strategies, and security protocols.

Permitting and Approvals (6–18 months): Navigating complex zoning regulations, building permits, environmental assessments, and utility connection approvals.

Construction and Infrastructure Installation (12–24 months): Often requiring sophisticated construction methods, specialized subcontractors, and rigorous compliance to exacting standards.

Equipment Installation, Testing, and Commissioning (6–12 months): Installation of advanced computing equipment, networking infrastructure, power systems, extensive testing, and verification before going live.

Electrical Consumption

Data centers are exceptionally power-intensive facilities, with electricity consumption levels comparable to small cities. Just a decade ago, a 20-megawatt (MW) data center was considered sizable. Today, facilities consuming hundreds of megawatts are commonplace, and the largest hyperscale data centers now exceed capacities of over 1 gigawatt (GW), a remarkable increase reflecting the explosive demand for digital services.

Common Hurdles and Obstacles

Developing data centers involves overcoming numerous obstacles, including:

Power and Infrastructure Availability: Securing sufficient power often requires extensive coordination with utility companies, which may need to upgrade or extend power grids, involving significant expense and delay.

Regulatory and Zoning Challenges: Many jurisdictions lack clear regulations tailored to data centers, leading to prolonged approval processes. Community opposition based on concerns related to noise, security, environmental impact, and heavy infrastructure needs can further complicate approvals.

Rising Construction Costs and Material Shortages: Increasing demand for data centers globally has led to escalating construction costs, labor shortages, and scarcity in key materials and components (such as transformers, generators, and specialized HVAC equipment).

Environmental Concerns and Sustainability Goals: Heightened scrutiny on energy consumption has increased the pressure on developers to meet stringent environmental and sustainability standards, adding to complexity and cost. This includes incorporating renewable energy sources and more efficient cooling systems to reduce carbon footprints.

Security and Cybersecurity: Cybersecurity threats and physical security risks demand elaborate security measures, access control systems, redundant backup protocols, and ongoing operational vigilance—each of which increases complexity and cost.

Despite these challenges, the immense and growing demand for reliable digital infrastructure continues to make data centers among the most valuable industrial assets.

Ultimately, developing and operating data centers is among the most technically demanding and intricate challenges in industrial real estate, requiring precision planning, substantial capital investment, and exceptional expertise to successfully navigate an increasingly complex landscape.

Figure 7: A large data center

Challenges in Developing TechFlex Properties

Power Accessibility: Securing sufficient power capacity or upgrading electrical infrastructure is time-consuming and costly.

Water Availability: Many regions lack infrastructure to meet the substantial water requirements, necessitating investment in recycling systems or locating near reliable water sources.

Location Constraints: Properties must balance access to resources, environmental stability, and transportation connectivity, carefully avoiding locations susceptible to disruptions (e.g., earthquakes).

Environmental Concerns: Resource-intensive operations face increased regulatory and community scrutiny, compelling developers to prioritize renewable energy, efficient design, and sustainable practices.

The Future of TechFlex Industrial

As industries like artificial intelligence, cloud computing, and electric vehicle production continue their rapid growth, the demand for specialized

TechFlex properties will only increase. Developers and investors who successfully navigate challenges related to power availability, site selection, and environmental considerations will be strategically positioned in this expanding sector.

Summary

TechFlex properties represent critical infrastructure supporting the world's most innovative industries. Understanding their unique power, water, and connectivity requirements enables industrial real estate stakeholders to effectively contribute to—and benefit from—the technological advancements driving future economic growth.

7

Land

THE DEVELOPMENT AND PREPARATION of land play a critical role in the success of industrial real estate projects. Transforming raw, undeveloped land into functional industrial space requires careful planning, substantial investment, and strict adherence to zoning and regulatory standards.

Raw Land vs. Developed Land

Industrial properties can originate as raw land, which requires extensive preparation before it becomes usable, including vegetation clearing, grading, compaction, and drainage management. In contrast, developed land typically includes existing infrastructure such as paved surfaces, utility connections, and zoning approvals, making it immediately ready for industrial use.

Site Preparation

Preparing industrial land involves several critical steps, including environmental assessments, soil testing, and engineering evaluations. Uneven terrain or poor soil conditions may necessitate stabilization methods such as importing fill or soil reinforcement. Regulatory compliance, including stormwater management, environmental impact assessments, and contamination control, is essential before development begins. Groundwater levels must also be assessed, as high water tables can affect site drainage and stability.

Geotechnical Reports

Geotechnical reports, often referred to as "Geotech reports," provide comprehensive evaluations of soil and subsurface conditions at a specific site.

Prepared by professional geotechnical engineers, these reports inform developers about soil composition, stability, groundwater levels, load-bearing capacity, and potential risks associated with construction.

Key components of a geotechnical report include:

- Soil Analysis: Detailed examination of soil type, density, moisture content, compaction, and potential contaminants.
- Load-Bearing Capacity: Recommendations on soil strength and suitability for supporting heavy structures, informing decisions about foundation types and construction methods.
- Groundwater Assessment: Identification of groundwater levels and potential drainage issues, which are crucial for designing effective stormwater management systems.
- Seismic and Geological Risks: Analysis of potential hazards such as seismic activity, landslides, subsidence, or expansive soils that could compromise structural integrity.
- Recommendations: Actionable guidance on ground stabilization, excavation methods, foundation requirements, and site preparation strategies tailored to the site's specific geotechnical conditions.

Geotechnical reports are crucial for mitigating risks, ensuring regulatory compliance, and informing design decisions that ultimately affect project costs and timelines. Neglecting thorough geotechnical evaluations can lead to unforeseen complications, expensive remediation efforts, and delays.

Groundwork and Grading

Proper groundwork ensures land stability and readiness for infrastructure. This includes clearing obstructions like trees, rocks, and debris, followed by grading to establish a level and stable surface. Grading often involves cutting and filling to achieve optimal elevation and drainage. In regions prone to heavy rainfall, features such as retention ponds, engineered drainage channels, and compacted sub-base layers are critical to prevent erosion and flooding. Ground stabilization techniques like soil compaction, chemical treatments, and geotextile layers further enhance load-bearing capacity and durability.

Infrastructure and Utility Considerations

Fully functional industrial sites require essential infrastructure such as roads, drainage systems, and utility access. Reliable electricity, water, sewer, and telecommunications services are crucial.

Developers should assess utility availability and associated costs during site selection. Limited electrical capacity might require investment in transformers or dedicated substations to meet high-energy demands.

Offsite Development Levies, Fees, and Taxes

Developers must also consider offsite development levies and other fees or taxes imposed by municipalities to fund infrastructure projects and public amenities related to industrial development. Offsite levies typically contribute to the cost of roads, water and sewer infrastructure, drainage systems, and public services necessary to support the development.

Key points to consider include:

- **Offsite Levies**: Municipalities assess these fees based on land area, projected use, and expected infrastructure needs. Rates can vary significantly depending on the municipality and development scale.
- **Impact Fees**: These are fees assessed to mitigate the impacts of new developments on local infrastructure, such as traffic improvements, parks, and public facilities.
- **Development Charges**: Some jurisdictions impose development charges to cover costs associated with expanding infrastructure capacity to accommodate growth.
- **Property and Special Assessment Taxes**: Developers should evaluate property tax rates and potential special assessments, which may be levied to fund specific projects benefiting the property directly.

Importantly, municipalities treat these fees and taxes differently, with variations in definitions, calculation methods, and payment schedules. Confirming the applicable charges and requirements in advance through direct consultation with local authorities is prudent due diligence. Developers must budget carefully for these costs and engage with local authorities early to accurately assess financial implications and negotiate terms if possible.

Surface Materials and Load-Bearing Capacity

The choice of surface materials impacts usability and maintenance:

> Gravel: Cost-effective, flexible, but requires regular upkeep.
> Asphalt: Ideal for high-traffic areas due to smoothness and moderate durability.
> Reinforced Concrete: Offers superior durability and is suitable for heavy machinery and long-term stability.
> Permeable Pavement: Useful in managing stormwater runoff while maintaining stability.

Load-bearing capacity is critical for tenants handling heavy freight, machinery, or large-scale storage. Sites supporting significant weight may require reinforced concrete pads or deep foundations to prevent subsidence or structural damage.

Land Valuation and Cost Factors

Industrial land value depends on location, zoning, infrastructure availability, and market demand. Sites near major transportation routes, ports, or intermodal hubs command premium prices. Additional cost factors include impact fees, property taxes, and site preparation expenses. Comprehensive due diligence and financial modeling help investors determine if a property aligns with their investment objectives.

Environmental and Zoning Regulations

Adhering to zoning laws and environmental regulations is crucial. Sites with past contamination may require remediation. Developers must navigate permitted uses, setback requirements, environmental protections, and regulations on emissions, noise, runoff, and hazardous materials.

Potential Risks and Challenges

Industrial land development faces various challenges:

- High land costs and permitting delays.

- Infrastructure limitations and environmental remediation.
- Market fluctuations, evolving industrial space demands, and regulatory changes.

Investors must anticipate these risks and incorporate contingency plans in their strategies.

Best Practices for Tenants and Investors

Tenants and investors should conduct thorough site evaluations, collaborate with experienced brokers, and consult zoning experts for compliance assurance. Analyzing market trends, infrastructure plans, and lease structures provides competitive advantages. Tenants should carefully review lease terms, including renewal options and expansion potential. Investors benefit from diversifying across various industrial land types to manage risks and optimize returns.

Summary

Effective land development is critical to industrial real estate success. Understanding land preparation, geotechnical conditions, infrastructure requirements, regulatory compliance, offsite levies, fees, and strategic valuation is essential for maximizing investment outcomes. Thorough evaluation and strategic management of development challenges enable tenants and investors to secure profitable, long-term industrial sites.

8

Site Selection

SELECTING THE OPTIMAL LOCATION is pivotal to the functionality and long-term success of industrial real estate projects. A well-chosen site enhances operational efficiency, tenant appeal, and property value, whereas a poorly selected location can result in ongoing operational challenges and reduced returns. Key considerations include infrastructure access, zoning, utilities, workforce availability, and market dynamics.

Expert Insight

"Great buildings attract great customers when they're in great locations. If you don't meet that standard, you're not going to get the kind of value that you want for your investors. If you invest in lesser quality properties, you have to ask yourself—are you truly getting paid enough to take that risk?"
—Douglas Kiersey, CEO & President of Dermody

Logistical and Supply Chain Considerations

Industrial properties benefit greatly from proximity to essential infrastructure—highways, railroads, ports, and airports—as well as to key suppliers and customers. Efficient infrastructure significantly reduces transportation costs and transit times, enhancing operational efficiency and reliability. For instance, distribution centers near major population centers can drastically reduce last-mile delivery costs, while manufacturing facilities close to suppliers can minimize production delays through reliable just-in-time (JIT) delivery systems.

Zoning and Permits

Ensuring a property is appropriately zoned for industrial activities is critical. A thorough understanding of local zoning regulations and permitting requirements helps prevent costly delays and ensures compliance with municipal standards. For example, a seemingly ideal urban site may face extensive zoning restrictions, complicating and prolonging the development process.

Access to Utilities

Reliable utilities—including electricity, water, natural gas, and high-speed internet—are foundational for industrial operations. Facilities like data centers and semiconductor fabs demand substantial and uninterrupted access to these utilities, particularly power and water. Insufficient power infrastructure might necessitate costly investments in transformers or substations, significantly impacting a project's budget and timeline.

Workforce Availability

Proximity to a skilled workforce is vital, especially for manufacturing and high-tech industries. Facilities benefit from nearby labor markets, educational institutions, and public transit options, reducing recruitment and commuting challenges, enhancing employee reliability, and possibly qualifying for government incentives. For instance, a manufacturing firm might choose a higher-cost site near public transit to reduce turnover and recruitment expenses.

Case Study: Site Selection for a Semiconductor Manufacturing Facility

A leading semiconductor manufacturer sought a location for a new, advanced fabrication plant. After evaluating several sites, they selected a 75-acre location that provided reliable infrastructure, including robust power, water supply, and high-speed fiber optic connectivity. The site offered environmental stability with minimal seismic and flood risks, essential for precise manufacturing operations. Proximity to technical universities and a skilled workforce, combined with streamlined permitting processes and attractive economic incentives, further enhanced the site's appeal.

This strategic choice accelerated project completion by six months, improved workforce recruitment and retention, and ensured uninterrupted operational reliability. Ultimately, the decision significantly boosted the company's competitive position and market share, highlighting the critical importance of thorough site selection for high-tech industrial facilities.

Physical and Environmental Considerations

Site characteristics and local environmental conditions significantly impact operational suitability. Factors such as site size, shape, and configuration must align with operational requirements, including sufficient space for buildings, parking, truck maneuvering, and future expansions. Additionally, environmental stability is critical, especially for sensitive operations. Sites prone to earthquakes, flooding, hurricanes, or even minor vibrations may require specialized construction techniques or structural reinforcements.

Cost Factors

Land prices, taxes, and development costs vary greatly. Prime urban locations typically command premium prices, reflecting excellent infrastructure and market proximity. Conversely, rural areas offer cost savings but may lack critical amenities. Investors should anticipate hidden expenses such as unexpected site remediation, infrastructure upgrades (like electrical substations), or compliance-related delays. A lower initial cost may not translate into long-term savings if operational efficiencies and expansion capabilities are compromised.

Specialized Considerations for High-Tech Facilities

Facilities in advanced sectors like data centers, gigafactories, and semiconductor fabs require special attention to:

Power Availability: Reliable access to high-capacity electricity is critical.
Water Resources: Large-scale industrial operations demand substantial and dependable water sources.
Network Connectivity: Robust, redundant internet infrastructure ensures operational continuity.

Balancing Priorities

No location will perfectly meet all criteria, making prioritization crucial.

For example:

Distribution Centers often prioritize proximity to highways and intermodal facilities to optimize logistics.

Semiconductor Fabs emphasize environmental stability, reliable power, and water resources to maintain operational integrity.

Manufacturing Plants generally focus on affordable land, skilled labor availability, and local incentives to ensure sustainable long-term operations. Carefully aligning these priorities with tenant needs is essential for successful industrial site selection.

Case Study: A Logistics Hub

A strategically located 50-acre site near a major interstate and within 10 miles of a rail terminal was selected following thorough data-driven analysis, including GIS mapping, traffic studies, and economic forecasts. The location provided direct highway access, proximity to rail and ports, ample space for growth, streamlined local zoning and permitting, availability of a skilled labor pool, and significant local tax incentives.

This strategic choice proved highly successful, achieving 90% occupancy within the first year. Tenants benefited from a 15% reduction in freight costs due to the site's strategic position, while the flexible layout allowed the facility to adapt quickly to evolving market demands.

Summary

Effective site selection underpins the success of industrial real estate projects. By rigorously evaluating factors such as infrastructure access, zoning, utilities, workforce availability, and market conditions, stakeholders can ensure their properties meet tenant requirements and achieve long-term profitability and competitiveness.

9

Logistics and Supply Chain Management

LOGISTICS AND SUPPLY CHAIN management are critical to the functionality of industrial real estate, optimizing the movement and storage of goods from manufacturers to consumers. Effective logistics ensures timely, cost-efficient delivery, making strategic use of warehouses, distribution centers, and transportation networks to meet growing consumer demands.

Role of Industrial Real Estate in Logistics

Industrial properties serve as pivotal nodes in the supply chain, enabling efficient storage, sorting, and distribution. The strategic placement of these properties is essential to managing logistics costs and meeting delivery expectations.

Expert Insight

"The new normal is disruption. We need optionality, not optimality. Optimality works if you know exactly what's going to happen, but today we never know what's coming next. Optionality is about having multiple scenarios ready, so when conditions change, you can quickly pivot and adapt."
— Dr. Jim Tompkins, Founder of Tompkins Ventures, LLC

Key Components of Logistics and Supply Chain Management

Transportation Infrastructure: Proximity to highways, ports, railroads, and airports significantly influences property value by reducing transit times and logistics expenses.

Inventory Management: Precise inventory control, aided by technologies like automated racking and real-time tracking systems, enhances operational efficiency.

Cold Chain Logistics: Facilities designed for temperature-sensitive goods must maintain strict environmental controls, crucial for sectors like food and pharmaceuticals.

Last-Mile and Middle-Mile Logistics

The complexity of logistics often centers around two critical segments:

Last-Mile Delivery: The final leg of the supply chain, it is cost-intensive due to factors like urban congestion and demand for rapid delivery. Strategically located urban fulfillment centers mitigate these challenges by minimizing distances and supporting rapid turnaround.

Middle-Mile Logistics: This involves transporting bulk goods between warehouses, regional hubs, and local distribution points. Efficiency in this stage relies on optimized freight transportation—primarily via trucks, rail, and air transport—to ensure a steady inventory flow and reduce overall logistics costs.

Expert Insight

"Last mile is a broad brush. It's not just the final step to the consumer's home— it's about minimizing the overall costs in your supply chain. That could mean being closer to a port, labor pools, or key logistics arteries. Ultimately, last mile means saving on the key cost drivers: transportation, labor, and inventory."
— Sean Dalfen, CEO of Dalfen Industrial

Challenges and Innovations in Logistics

Logistics operations face ongoing pressures, including fuel costs, driver shortages, and fluctuating freight rates. Companies are increasingly adopting innovative solutions such as:

Electric and Autonomous Vehicles: These technologies aim to reduce operational costs and environmental impacts.

Predictive Analytics: Leveraging AI and data analytics helps companies anticipate demand fluctuations and optimize inventory management.

Intermodal Transport: Combining trucking with rail or air transport increases efficiency, especially for middle-mile logistics.

Trends Transforming Logistics and Supply Chains

Key industry trends reshaping logistics include:

E-Commerce Expansion: Accelerated online shopping demands strategically placed fulfillment centers near population centers to support fast delivery.

Automation and Technology: Robotics, AI, and IoT are transforming inventory management, picking, packing, and shipping processes, significantly improving speed and accuracy.

Sustainability: A shift toward green logistics has led to investments in renewable energy, electric vehicles, and energy-efficient facilities.

Resilience: Post-pandemic strategies prioritize supply chain resilience through nearshoring, diversified supplier networks, and buffer inventory management.

Strategic Location Selection for Logistics Properties

Site selection for logistics properties must consider:

Population Proximity: Facilities near urban centers optimize last-mile delivery efficiency.

Multimodal Transportation Access: Properties near intermodal terminals facilitate seamless goods transfer between transportation modes.

Scalability: Sites designed for expansion and adaptation to changing logistics demands offer significant competitive advantages.

Labor Availability: Access to skilled, cost-effective labor is crucial for operational success, particularly in labor-intensive tasks.

Challenges in Logistics and Supply Chain Management

Operators face several challenges:

Cost Pressure: Rising transportation and labor expenses demand efficiency optimization.

Space Constraints: High competition for strategic locations has led to space shortages and higher lease rates.

Environmental Compliance: Stricter sustainability regulations require significant investment in eco-friendly technologies.

Case Study: A High-Performance Fulfillment Center

A 500,000-square-foot fulfillment center strategically positioned near a major metropolitan area showcases the successful integration of advanced logistics and innovative practices. Its proximity to major highways and transportation hubs significantly reduces transit times, boosting both middle-mile and last-mile efficiency. The facility leverages cutting-edge automation, including AI-driven robotics and automated storage systems, streamlining inventory management to enhance order accuracy and reduce labor requirements. Additionally, the building's flexible, high-bay design maximizes storage capacity and allows rapid adaptation to shifting market demands.

Operationally, the fulfillment center achieves exceptional efficiency by enabling next-day and same-day deliveries, thus effectively meeting consumer expectations in a competitive market. Its investments in advanced automation have reduced labor dependency by approximately 30%, while sustainability initiatives, such as solar power, LED lighting, EV charging stations, and energy-efficient HVAC systems, have lowered energy consumption by 20%. This fulfillment center exemplifies how strategic site selection, technological advancement, and sustainable practices together provide significant competitive advantages in today's evolving logistics landscape.

Summary

Efficient logistics and effective supply chain management are critical drivers of demand for industrial real estate. As customer expectations grow and technology advances, strategically located, adaptable, and sustainable industrial properties will become increasingly valuable. Stakeholders who understand these dynamics are well-positioned to succeed in this evolving market.

10

Zoning

ZONING MAY NOT IMMEDIATELY seem exciting, but it is critical to understanding and successfully navigating industrial real estate. Zoning regulations define permissible activities on properties, guiding industrial development and safeguarding community interests. Failing to grasp zoning nuances can result in costly mistakes, delays, or disputes.

Understanding Zoning

Zoning refers to municipal regulations governing property use within specific areas. Municipalities divide land into various zones—such as residential, commercial, industrial, agricultural, or mixed-use—and establish rules for building types, permissible activities, and property characteristics, including heights, setbacks, and parking requirements.

Simply put, zoning determines what activities are allowed on specific parcels of land. For industrial properties, zoning distinctions (like light industrial versus heavy industrial) determine operational suitability, affecting everything from manufacturing processes to logistics.

Key Components of Zoning

Zoning Districts: Municipalities categorize land into zones, each with unique regulatory criteria.
Zoning Ordinances: Written laws detailing specific rules for each zone, including:
Permitted Uses: Allowed activities or businesses.
Building Heights and Setbacks: Limits on structure dimensions and positioning relative to property lines.
Density and Floor Area Ratio (FAR): Restrictions on building size and usage intensity.

Parking Requirements: Mandated number of parking spaces relative to property use.

Special Permits and Variances: Mechanisms allowing exceptions to standard zoning regulations if the proposed changes are deemed beneficial or harmless.

Zoning Maps: Graphical depictions identifying zoning boundaries within a municipality, crucial for development planning and compliance.

Figure 8: A zoning map showing different classifications

Historical Perspective on Industrial Zoning

Historically, zoning has been employed primarily to isolate industrial properties from residential areas, minimizing conflicts arising from noise, pollution, traffic, and other nuisances. However, as cities evolve, once-clear boundaries have begun to blur. Urban expansion, adaptive reuse of industrial spaces, and the rise of mixed-use developments have prompted municipalities to reassess—and sometimes soften—zoning boundaries to accommodate economic growth and changing community needs.

Importance of Zoning Compatibility and Business Licensing

Every business, upon applying for a business license, receives a municipal-assigned **use classification**. This classification must match or be fully compatible with the property's zoning to obtain a business license.

For instance, consider a logistics company purchasing an industrial-zoned property for warehousing and trucking. While warehousing might be permitted, overnight truck storage could be explicitly prohibited. Since their primary business classification involves "trucking and logistics," the municipality could deny their business license application, jeopardizing operations, leading to financial losses, legal costs, and significant operational disruption.

Conditional Uses, Special Exceptions, and Variances

Zoning flexibility is sometimes available through mechanisms like Conditional Use Permits or special variances. These allow deviations from standard regulations but typically require extensive applications, public hearings, and community engagement. Approval processes can be lengthy, costly, and uncertain.

For example, a machining business wishing to operate in a 'light industrial' zone—typically excluding heavy metalworking due to noise and vibration—must apply for a conditional use permit. They must demonstrate comprehensive mitigation measures to overcome community concerns, facing intense scrutiny and potential opposition.

Non-Conforming Uses ("Grandfathering")

When zoning regulations change, existing uses may become legally non-conforming (or "grandfathered"), allowing operations to continue under current ownership. However, significant restrictions typically apply, limiting expansions, renovations, or property improvements. This status can severely impact future property values and marketability, presenting challenges to both current owners and future buyers.

Rezoning Applications and Implications

Rezoning properties is possible but challenging. Applications involve political processes, public hearings, and often face community opposition. Such processes may significantly delay or derail intended projects.

Consider a developer acquiring industrial land intending to build mixed-use residential and retail spaces. Miscalculating rezoning timelines could delay the project by years, negatively affecting project viability, funding arrangements, and overall profitability.

Municipal Enforcement and Consequences of Zoning Violations

Municipalities actively enforce zoning compliance through inspections, complaints, and investigations. Operating contrary to zoning rules—even unintentionally—can lead to serious repercussions, including:

- Substantial fines
- Cease-and-desist orders
- Mandated property modifications
- Forced business relocations
- Legal actions and reputational damage

Overlay Districts and Supplemental Regulations

Some properties fall within special overlay districts (e.g., airport flight paths, historic areas, floodplains, environmentally sensitive zones) imposing additional restrictions beyond standard zoning ordinances. For instance, an industrial site near an airport may face restrictions on building height or noise levels, significantly affecting permissible uses, renovations, and future expansions.

Real-World Examples

Negative Example: A company invests substantially to convert a warehouse into a woodworking facility without confirming zoning compatibility. When applying for a business license, they discover woodworking violates zoning rules, forcing expensive retrofits, lengthy zoning applications, or relocation.

Positive Example: Another company proactively engages city planners, securing a variance to transform an outdated manufacturing warehouse into a vibrant flex-industrial retail and office facility. Early community engagement and municipal collaboration paved the way for timely approvals and a successful project.

Zoning Varies Considerably by Market

It's critical to recognize zoning regulations vary significantly across markets. For example, Houston, Texas, famously lacks traditional zoning ordinances.

Instead, Houston relies on market-driven factors, minimal regulatory tools such as deed restrictions and land-use covenants, and a laissez-faire approach to development control. While this flexible system fosters diverse land uses and rapid development, it can also result in unpredictable neighborhood compositions and land-use conflicts.

By contrast, other cities, such as those in California or the Northeastern U.S., have highly detailed, restrictive zoning laws designed to precisely control property use, height, density, and even aesthetics. Understanding these local differences is vital when exploring or expanding into new industrial markets.

Case Study: Rollercoaster Conflict in Kemah, Texas

In Kemah, Texas—a city known for its lack of formal zoning regulations— a significant conflict arose when the Kemah Boardwalk constructed a large wooden roller coaster called the Boardwalk Bullet, merely 200 feet from residential properties. Neighbors, who had no prior notice or input, raised immediate concerns regarding noise, vibrations, and impacts on property values.

Despite objections, the city administrator confirmed that no special permits or public hearings were required since Kemah has no zoning laws, and all setback requirements had been met. Residents considered legal action but ultimately chose not to proceed due to concerns about the cost and difficulty of opposing a large commercial entity.

This case highlights the challenges that can emerge in cities without clear zoning frameworks, underscoring the tension between commercial development and residential quality of life.

Why Zoning Matters

Zoning fulfills critical community and economic roles:

- Protects communities by separating incompatible uses (e.g., heavy industry from residential or educational areas).
- Preserves and stabilizes property values by regulating land use.
- Facilitates efficient infrastructure planning and protects environmental resources.

Future Trends in Zoning

Emerging zoning trends include:

Mixed-Use Zoning: Encouraging developments combining industrial, commercial, and residential uses, creating more dynamic urban environments.

Adaptive Reuse: Municipalities increasingly support repurposing older industrial buildings into modern, multipurpose facilities.

Technological Influence: The rapid growth of technology-driven industries (such as e-commerce and data centers) is prompting municipalities to revisit and update zoning codes.

Practical Steps for Navigating Zoning

To mitigate zoning risks, follow these practical steps:

Verify Local Regulations: Review municipal zoning ordinances carefully; no two markets are identical.

Confirm Compatibility: Explicitly confirm the municipality's assigned business-use classification aligns fully with property zoning.

Zoning Verification Letters: Obtain written verification from municipalities before finalizing transactions.

Contract Safeguards: Ensure purchase or lease agreements include clauses contingent upon obtaining zoning and business licensing approval.

Engage Professionals Early: Consult zoning specialists, local attorneys, or planning professionals proactively to navigate complexities.

Summary

Zoning is foundational—not optional—to successful industrial real estate transactions. A clear understanding of municipal regulations, proactive due diligence, and professional assistance help avoid costly pitfalls and smooth the path to profitable and compliant industrial projects. Taking zoning seriously from the outset can mean the difference between success and costly failure in industrial real estate.

11

Measurements

ACCURATE MEASUREMENTS are crucial in industrial real estate, influencing pricing, leasing terms, building functionality, and regulatory compliance. Understanding the nuances of property measurements ensures transparency, facilitates efficient decision-making, and prevents costly errors.

Pricing per Square Foot

Industrial properties are typically marketed based on price per square foot, with variations by market:

Per Annum: Most regions calculate rent annually (e.g., $10 per sq. ft. per annum).
Per Month: Certain markets, such as parts of California, use monthly pricing (e.g., $0.83 per sq. ft. per month).

Clearly understanding your local market's pricing convention is critical for accurate budgeting and comparisons. A building's size directly influences its valuation and rental terms, making precise measurements vital.

Measurement Standards

The prevailing standard for measuring industrial buildings is the BOMA 2025 for Industrial Buildings Standard Method of Measurement (ANSI/BOMA Z65.2-2025). Developed by the Building Owners and Managers Association (BOMA) in collaboration with the Society of Industrial and Office Realtors (SIOR), this standard provides consistency and comparability in square footage calculations, enhancing accuracy across transactions.

Floor Plans and Documentation

Accurate documentation is fundamental to industrial real estate transactions and operations. Key types include:

CADD Files: Digital, scalable representations detailing building layouts.
As-Built Drawings: Depict actual conditions post-construction, capturing modifications or adjustments.
Engineered Drawings: Technical specifications highlighting structural integrity, load-bearing capacities, and construction materials.
Architectural Drawings: Detail design and aesthetic aspects of the building.

Each drawing type serves distinct purposes and is essential for accurate property assessment, leasing negotiations, and due diligence.

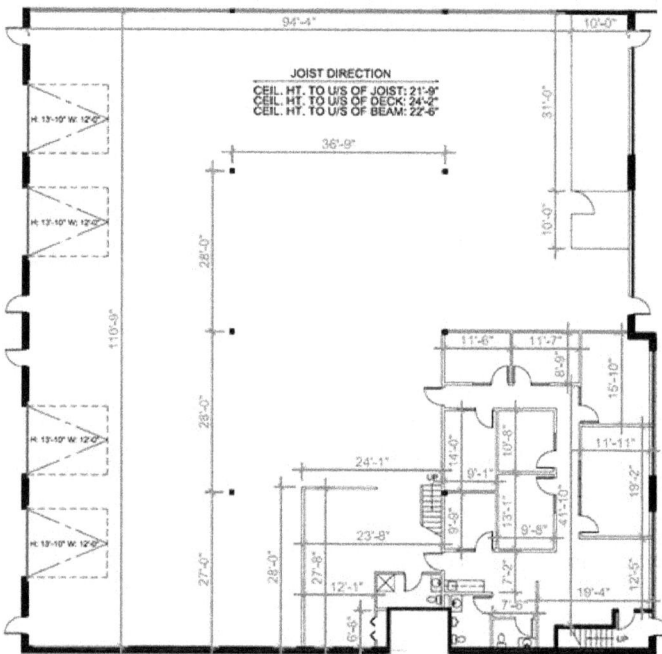

Figure 9: A floor plan with measurements

Mezzanine vs. Second Floor Space

Recognizing distinctions between mezzanine and second-floor spaces is important due to varying implications for rent and compliance:

Second-Floor Space: Fully enclosed, typically with dedicated HVAC, electrical systems, and access points.
Usually requires fire-rated walls for compliance.
Commonly considered rentable square footage.
Mezzanine Space: Internally accessed, often open and not fully enclosed.
Typically used for supplementary storage or office functions. Generally, not included in rentable area unless constructed to high standards (e.g., steel/concrete).

Market conditions influence mezzanine rentability; landlords in tight markets may charge for mezzanine space, whereas tenants may resist such charges in softer markets. Older industrial buildings often have unpermitted or poorly constructed mezzanines, emphasizing the need for thorough inspections and compliance verification.

Figure 10: An example of mezzanine space

Usable vs. Rentable Square Footage

Although far less common in industrial compared to office spaces, distinguishing between usable and rentable square footage can occasionally arise, particularly in flex properties:

Usable Square Footage: Actual tenant-occupied space, excluding common areas.

Rentable Square Footage: Usable space plus a proportional share of common areas (e.g., lobbies, corridors), known as the load factor.

Understanding these terms helps prevent misunderstandings in lease negotiations and ensures clarity in rent calculations.

Important Measurement Terminology

Gross Building Area (GBA): Total floor area of a building, including all interior and exterior walls.

Gross Leasable Area (GLA): Area intended for exclusive use by tenants, typically excluding common areas.

Net Leasable Area (NLA): Actual usable space available for tenant occupancy, excluding common and service areas.

Impact of Inaccurate Measurements

Inaccurate or misleading measurements can have significant financial and legal consequences. For instance, a property advertised at 100,000 sq. ft. that measures only 95,000 sq. ft. could lead to disputes over rent, potential lease terminations, or even litigation, highlighting the need for meticulous accuracy.

Measurement Verification Methods

To ensure measurement accuracy, stakeholders commonly engage third-party measurement specialists who employ methods such as laser scanning, physical surveys, or advanced 3D imaging technologies. These independent assessments verify measurements, helping avoid disputes and discrepancies.

Real-World Example: Measurement Dispute

A tenant leased a building marketed at 150,000 sq. ft. but later discovered it measured approximately 142,000 sq. ft. This discrepancy led to a renegotiation of lease terms and financial compensation for overpaid rent, demonstrating the critical importance of verifying building measurements upfront.

Common Pitfalls and Best Practices

- Always confirm measurement standards used in property marketing and leases.
- Obtain accurate floor plans and documentation early to prevent disputes.
- Conduct due diligence on mezzanine and second-floor spaces to verify compliance and structural integrity.
- Clearly define and understand rentable versus usable areas in lease agreements.
- Engage independent measurement specialists to validate square footage claims.

Summary

Precise measurements underpin effective industrial real estate management, influencing valuations, lease terms, and functional efficiency. Familiarity with measurement standards, accurate documentation, and awareness of market-specific practices help stakeholders make informed decisions, maximizing property value and minimizing risk.

12

Architecture and Design

INDUSTRIAL ARCHITECTURE BLENDS functional design principles with operational demands, enhancing efficiency, flexibility, worker experience, and sustainability. This chapter explores critical architectural considerations, emerging trends, and their impact on industrial real estate performance.

Form Follows Function

Industrial architecture is driven primarily by practicality, yet thoughtful design simultaneously boosts efficiency, safety, and aesthetics. Buildings must support current operations and anticipate future growth.

Factories & Manufacturing Facilities

Manufacturing facilities require specialized layouts optimized for material flow, production efficiency, and worker safety:

- Large, open spaces with minimal interior columns.
- Reinforced flooring for heavy machinery and equipment.
- High ceilings for cranes, ventilation, and specialized equipment.
- Advanced MEP systems for compressed air, water, and waste disposal.
- Zoned layouts separating raw materials, production, and finished goods.
- Safety compliance with regulatory standards.

Design Considerations:

- Flow optimization for efficient assembly processes.

- Modular design allowing easy future expansions.
- Enhanced environmental controls for ventilation and noise reduction.

Warehouses & Distribution Centers

Efficient movement of goods makes warehouse design vital:

- Clear-span structures maximizing storage and operational flexibility.
- High dock ratios for rapid shipment handling.
- Automation compatibility (AS/RS, robotic picking).
- Efficient truck courts and trailer circulation.
- Clear heights of 32'–40' or higher.
- Multi-temperature zones for specialized storage.

Design Considerations:

- Cross-docking for efficient goods transfer.
- Climate-controlled spaces for perishable goods.
- Urban logistics centers tailored for rapid last-mile delivery.
- IoT-enabled inventory and logistics management.

Flex Industrial Spaces

Flex buildings integrate office, industrial, and retail spaces within versatile layouts:

- Mixed-use layouts combining offices, assembly, and storage.
- Modular configurations supporting scalable operations.
- Enhanced aesthetics with contemporary facades and customer-facing design.
- Higher parking ratios accommodating diverse employee roles.

Design Considerations:

- Lower ceilings (16'–24') compared to traditional warehouses.
- Access points such as dock-high doors and drive-in bays.
- Variable office-to-warehouse ratios tailored to tenants.

TechFlex (Powered Industrial)

- TechFlex properties address high-tech industries' demands, like data centers and gigafactories, requiring significant power and advanced infrastructure:
- High-powered electrical infrastructure for intensive energy usage.
- Advanced cooling and water management systems.
- Seismic and climate-resilient structures.
- Secure data infrastructure for sensitive operations.
- Mixed-use spaces combining cleanrooms, manufacturing, and offices.

Design Considerations:

- Specialized utilities (high power, redundant backups).
- Security enhancements (biometric access, controlled zones).
- Flexible infrastructure adaptable to technological advancements.

Efficiency in Layouts

Optimized layouts enhance operational efficiency and workflow:

- Clear-span structures maximize flexible use.
- Strategically placed loading docks reduce bottlenecks.
- Integrated office spaces separated effectively from operational areas.
- Good design prioritizes movement efficiency for both workers and machinery.

Sustainability in Industrial Architecture

- Sustainable features reduce operational costs and environmental impact:
- Daylighting via skylights and clerestory windows.
- High-performance insulation reducing energy usage.
- Renewable energy solutions (solar panels, green roofs).
- Water conservation through rainwater harvesting and low-flow fixtures.

Materials and Flexibility

Modern industrial buildings balance durability with adaptability:

- Steel and concrete for structural strength.
- Glass for daylighting and aesthetics.
- Pre-insulated panels for energy efficiency and rapid installation.
- Flexible design elements like modular layouts and demountable partitions accommodate changing tenant needs.

Worker-Centric Design

Improving worker conditions enhances productivity and retention:

- Climate-controlled environments.
- Efficient LED and natural lighting.
- Ergonomic and comfortable workspaces.

Specialized Spaces: Mezzanines and Multi-Level Designs

Secondary spaces optimize building usage:

Mezzanines: Cost-effective, additional storage or office space without footprint expansion.
Second Floors: Fully enclosed, suitable for offices, labs, or specialized functions, maximizing vertical space.

The Future of Industrial Architecture

Emerging trends shaping industrial buildings:

Net-Zero & Sustainable Design: Solar integration, energy storage, and high-efficiency systems.
Automation-Ready Facilities: Infrastructure adapted for autonomous vehicles, drones, robotics, and IoT connectivity.
Blending Industrial & Office Environments: Integrating modern office amenities, hybrid spaces, and employee-focused design.

Architectural Influences and Innovations

Historical architects like Albert Kahn, Walter Gropius, and Peter Behrens set foundational principles of industrial architecture, emphasizing practicality, innovation, and aesthetics, influencing modern facility design.

Summary

Effective industrial architecture aligns practical function with innovative design. As industry evolves, architecture must anticipate technological advancements, sustainability demands, and workforce needs. The thoughtful integration of operational efficiency, flexibility, and environmental stewardship ensures industrial buildings remain valuable, functional, and future-proof assets.

13

Construction

UNDERSTANDING THE CONSTRUCTION elements of an industrial property is crucial for evaluating its value, functionality, and durability. Whether you are new to the industry or have years of experience, knowing what makes up a building and how its components interact with the land is fundamental. This chapter provides a comprehensive guide to construction in industrial real estate, focusing on structural elements, key interior systems, water management, and land upgrades.

Overall Principles of Building Construction

The foundation of industrial construction lies in the core principles that guide the process. These principles ensure that buildings are not only functional but also safe, efficient, and adaptable to the evolving needs of their users.

Functionality and Purpose

Every industrial building is designed with a specific purpose in mind, and construction must align with that purpose. For example:

- Manufacturing Facilities: Require high power capacity, durable flooring, and clear spans for machinery.
- Warehousing: Prioritize vertical space, dock access, and efficient material flow.
- Distribution Centers: Focus on accessibility, large truck courts, and rapid loading/unloading capabilities.
- Accessibility for commercial vehicles and

Safety and Compliance

Safety is paramount in construction. Buildings must adhere to local building codes, zoning regulations, and safety standards.

- Structural Integrity: Ensuring the building can withstand loads, environmental stresses, and operational wear.
- Fire Safety: Integrating fire suppression systems, safe evacuation routes, and fire-resistant materials.
- Worker Safety: Proper lighting, ventilation, and ergonomic design promote a safe working environment.

Fire Alarm Systems

Fire alarm systems are a crucial component of industrial building safety. These systems include smoke and heat detectors, manual pull stations, audible alarms, and automated notification systems to alert occupants and emergency personnel in case of fire. Industrial facilities often require high-sensitivity smoke detectors, especially in areas where dust, fumes, or chemicals could impact fire detection.

Many modern fire alarm systems are integrated with fire suppression systems and building management systems to provide real-time monitoring and automated emergency response. Compliance with National Fire Protection Association (NFPA) / National Research Council of Canada (NRC) codes and local regulations is essential to ensure that fire alarm systems are properly designed, installed, and maintained.

In addition, redundancy and backup power sources should be incorporated to ensure system reliability in case of electrical failures. Routine testing and maintenance are necessary to keep fire alarm systems operational, ensuring they function properly during an emergency.

Durability and Longevity

Industrial buildings are significant investments, and their construction must ensure durability over decades of use.

- Material Selection: Using high-quality, resilient materials like reinforced concrete and steel.
- Maintenance Access: Designing for easy access to key systems like HVAC, plumbing, and electrical for repairs and upgrades.

- Weather Resistance: Addressing regional challenges like heavy snow, high winds, or intense heat.

Cost Considerations

Balancing cost efficiency in industrial construction is essential for both initial investment and long-term operational savings.

- Initial Costs: Materials, labor, and specialized systems can drive up initial expenses. Compare costs of materials like steel versus concrete, or asphalt versus concrete for paving, based on long-term durability.
- Budget Planning: A phased construction plan can help manage upfront costs while maintaining quality.
- Capital Costs vs. Operational Costs (lifecycle & maintenance costs): One of the most overlooked aspects of industrial real estate construction is the balance between capital costs and operational costs. While lower upfront costs may seem appealing, they can often result in higher long-term expenses due to maintenance, energy inefficiencies, and frequent repairs. Evaluating the total lifecycle cost of ownership is essential when making construction decisions.
  - i. Lifecycle Costs: The total cost of ownership extends beyond just initial construction. It includes maintenance, energy usage, and repair frequency. For example, while LED lighting and high-quality roofing materials may come with a higher upfront cost, they often result in substantial savings over time due to lower energy consumption and reduced maintenance. Similarly, investing in insulated roofing, advanced HVAC systems, and modern fire suppression technologies can significantly lower long-term expenses by improving efficiency and durability.
  - ii. Preventive Maintenance & Long-Term Value: Choosing high-quality materials and systems at the outset minimizes the need for costly replacements. Regular maintenance schedules and using durable materials like reinforced concrete and industrial-grade steel can prevent significant repair costs and downtime in operations.

Factoring in future expansion needs and modular construction options can also reduce capital expenditures in the long run by making properties adaptable to changing tenant demands.

iii. Operational Efficiency & Tenant Appeal: A well-built industrial property with lower operating costs is more attractive to tenants and investors. Buildings with energy-efficient HVAC systems, optimized warehouse layouts, and sustainable infrastructure often command higher lease rates and longer tenant commitments. Industrial tenants are increasingly prioritizing properties that offer predictable utility costs and lower maintenance burdens, making the choice between capital and operational costs a strategic decision.

- Value Engineering: Collaborate with contractors, architects, and engineers to identify cost-saving measures without compromising functionality or safety.
- Scheduling & Timeline Management: Time is money in industrial real estate construction. Delays in procurement, permitting, or labor availability can significantly impact project costs and timelines. Using readily available materials and understanding lead times for specialized components ensures smoother project execution. Developers should work with suppliers and contractors to identify potential bottlenecks early and explore alternatives when certain materials face shortages. Additionally, establishing a phased construction schedule allows for portions of a facility to become operational while other areas are still under development, optimizing cash flow and tenant readiness.

Sustainability

Modern construction increasingly incorporates sustainable practices to reduce environmental impact and meet regulatory requirements.

- LEED Certification: Buildings certified for Leadership in Energy and Environmental Design (LEED) demonstrate sustainability.
- Recycled Materials: Using recycled steel, concrete, or other

materials where feasible.

- Water Conservation: Integrating rainwater harvesting, low-flow fixtures, and efficient drainage systems.

Accessibility for Commercial Vehicles & Employees

Proper accessibility is essential for industrial facilities, ensuring smooth operations for both commercial vehicles and employees.

Truck Access

Industrial properties must be designed to accommodate semi-trucks, delivery vehicles, and heavy-duty transport. This includes adequate turning radii, properly designed truck courts, and designated waiting areas to prevent congestion. Wide entry and exit points, reinforced pavement for heavy loads, and clear signage help improve the efficiency of vehicle flow. Loading doors should be strategically placed to minimize bottlenecks and maximize throughput, ensuring seamless freight movement.

Employee Access & Parking

For employees, accessibility considerations include well-designed parking areas, pedestrian walkways, and safe entry points. Sufficient on-site parking should be provided for both dayshift and night-shift workers, especially in locations with limited public transportation access. Sidewalks, crosswalks, and designated pedestrian zones improve safety in busy industrial sites where large vehicles operate.

Compliance with Accessibility Standards

Facilities should comply with ADA (Americans with Disabilities Act) standards in the U.S. or CSA accessibility standards in Canada, ensuring equal access for individuals with disabilities. This includes properly designed ramps, doorways, and interior layouts to accommodate mobility-impaired employees and visitors. Proper lighting, clear wayfinding signs, and emergency accessibility measures should also be integrated to create a safe and functional environment for all workers.

Flexibility and Adaptability

Industrial needs can change over time, and a building must be adaptable.

- Modular Design: Using modular components for easy reconfiguration.
- Universal Systems: Installing systems like HVAC and lighting that can accommodate changes in usage.
- Expansion Planning: Pre-planning for additional square footage, dock doors, or parking areas.

By adhering to these principles, construction projects can achieve optimal functionality, safety, and cost-efficiency, ensuring they meet the demands of both present and future users.

The Building Envelope

The building envelope refers to the structural elements and cladding that separate the interior from the exterior environment. It plays a critical role in maintaining the integrity of the property and ensuring its energy efficiency.

Walls

Industrial building walls are typically constructed using concrete, steel, masonry, or insulated metal panels, each with its own cost, durability, thermal efficiency, and fire resistance characteristics. The choice of wall material impacts construction speed, energy performance, maintenance requirements, and long-term operating costs.

Common Wall Materials

Industrial walls can be built from concrete, steel, masonry, or insulated metal panels. The choice affects construction speed, energy efficiency, and maintenance.

Wall Type	Pros	Cons	Best For
Precast Concrete	Fire-resistant, fast installation	Requires cranes, high transport costs	Warehouses, data centers
Tilt-Up Concrete	Cost-efficient, durable	Requires on-site space for casting	Distribution centers, manufacturing
Pre-Insulated Metal Panels	High insulation, lightweight	Susceptible to impact damage	Cold storage, energy-efficient buildings
Masonry / Concrete Block	Strong, impact-resistant	Labor-intensive, slow to build	High-impact areas like auto repair shops

Insulation and Fire Rating Considerations

Regardless of wall material, insulation and fire resistance play critical roles in building performance and regulatory compliance.

Insulation Options

- Spray Foam: High-performance air sealing but more expensive.
- Fiberglass or Mineral Wool: Cost-effective and fire-resistant.
- Rigid Insulation Boards: Commonly used with metal panels and concrete walls.

Fire Rating Requirements

- Concrete and masonry offer natural fire resistance.
- Steel and insulated metal panels may require fire barriers or coatings.
- Fire partitions and barriers may be required by code in multi-tenant industrial spaces.
- Consider fire ratings between different occupancy areas such as Warehouse, Office, Storage & Utility Rooms, etc.

Wall Systems and Weather Considerations

The choice of an industrial wall system is also heavily influenced by the climate and environmental conditions in which the facility operates. Temperature extremes, moisture exposure, wind resistance, and even seismic activity all play a role in determining which material will provide the best long-term performance. Below is a breakdown of how different wall systems perform in various environmental conditions.

Climate/Condition	Best Wall Materials	Why?
Cold Climates	Pre-Insulated Metal Panels, Tilt-Up Concrete, Precast Concrete	High insulation, resistance to freeze-thaw cycles
Hot/Dry Climates	Tilt-Up Concrete, Precast Concrete, Light-Colored Metal Panels	Reflects heat, maintains indoor temperature stability
Humid/Coastal	Precast Concrete, Tilt-Up Concrete, Sealed CMU, Coated Metal Panels	Resists moisture, corrosion, and mold growth
High Wind/Hurricanes	Tilt-Up Concrete, Precast Concrete, Reinforced Masonry	Withstands wind loads, impact-resistant
Seismic Zones	Precast Concrete with Reinforced Joints, Steel Panels, Tilt-Up Concrete with Bracing	Flexibility and structural resilience

Choosing the right industrial wall system depends on the location, budget, fire safety requirements, insulation needs, and construction timeline. Tilt-up concrete and precast concrete are ideal for large-scale, fire-resistant buildings, while pre-insulated metal panels provide a lightweight, energy-efficient alternative for temperature-sensitive facilities. Steel and masonry options cater to specific structural and durability needs, making it essential to evaluate long-term performance alongside initial costs.

Roof

Flat roofs with membrane systems are common, though pitched metal roofs may be used for durability and drainage. Built-Up Roofs are still common in many markets as well. Roofs are discussed in detail in Chapter 19: Roofs.

Floors

Industrial floors are almost always constructed from reinforced concrete due to its strength, durability, and load-bearing capacity. Standard floors are typically 6 inches thick, but certain industrial applications may require significantly thicker slabs.

- Standard Thickness (6 inches): Suitable for light-duty warehouses, distribution centers, and general storage facilities where loads are primarily from foot traffic, shelving, and standard forklifts.
- Heavy-Duty Thickness (6-8 inches): Required for facilities with constant forklift traffic, moderate racking loads, and light manufacturing.

- Extra Heavy-Duty Thickness (8-12 inches): Used in manufacturing plants, truck terminals, and facilities with heavy machinery where higher point loads are expected.
- Extreme Load Applications (12+ inches): Found in high-impact facilities such as steel mills, automotive plants, aircraft hangars, or facilities with automated storage retrieval systems (AS/RS). These floors may also incorporate post-tensioned concrete slabs to enhance durability and minimize cracking.

In addition to thickness, fiber reinforcement, rebar grids, and post-tensioning techniques can be used to improve the slab's structural integrity. Heavier loads or vibration-intensive operations may require denser concrete mixes or steel fiber reinforcement to prevent premature wear and cracking.

Load Rating

Industrial floors must be designed to support the specific demands of a facility, ensuring they can handle the required loads without failure or excessive wear. The suitability of a floor depends on its thickness, reinforcement, and subgrade preparation, all of which must be tailored to the intended use.

A floor built for light-duty applications, such as general storage or office space, may not be sufficient for warehouse racking, forklift traffic, or heavy machinery. While a floor that is overbuilt for its use may lead to unnecessary costs, an undersized or under-reinforced slab can cause significant structural issues, costly repairs, and operational disruptions.

For facilities with high-density storage, heavy equipment, or automated systems, a more robust slab may be required to prevent cracking, settlement, or long-term degradation. Boring and soil testing may also be necessary to assess subgrade conditions and ensure the foundation can support the anticipated loads.

Additionally, specialized applications, such as cold storage or environments with extreme temperature fluctuations, may require insulated or reinforced flooring to prevent issues related to expansion, contraction, and moisture intrusion.

Careful evaluation of floor requirements upfront is critical, as it is far easier to adjust for less intensive use than to remedy an inadequate slab after the facility is in operation.

Flatness and Levelness

For high-bay warehouses, racking systems, and automated facilities, floor flatness and levelness are critical to safety and operational efficiency. These factors are measured using FF (Flatness) and FL (Levelness) ratings, with higher numbers indicating greater precision. Note some scenarios this might also be measured in fractions of an inch (ex. 1/8") over 10 feet.

- FF 25 / FL 20: Standard warehouse floors with general forklift traffic.
- FF 35 / FL 25: Required for moderate racking systems and equipment-sensitive operations.
- FF 50+ / FL 50+: High-precision floors designed for automated retrieval systems, robotic operations, and laser-guided forklifts.

Floors with poor flatness can cause uneven loading, inefficient stacking, and excessive wear on material handling equipment, making these ratings particularly important for logistics and distribution centers.

Coatings and Surface Treatments

Floor coatings improve durability, safety, and resistance to wear. Common options include:

- Polished Concrete: Low-maintenance and highly resistant to abrasions, commonly used in high-traffic industrial settings.
- Sealed Concrete: Helps prevent moisture penetration and dust formation, often used in warehouses and cold storage.
- Anti-Static Coatings: Essential for electronics manufacturing and facilities with sensitive equipment.
- Facilities handling chemicals, heavy oils, or corrosive materials may require specialized coatings tailored to their industry needs.

Industrial concrete floors serve as the literal foundation for facility operations, and selecting the right thickness, reinforcement, and finish is critical. The decision should be based on load requirements, racking configurations, and future adaptability to avoid costly retrofits or premature degradation.

Key Interior Systems

Inside the building, several essential systems ensure functionality and compliance with regulations.

Electrical (see more in Chapter 18: Electrical)

- Power Requirements: Industrial buildings often require three-phase power for heavy equipment and advanced machinery. Voltage requirements should be assessed based on the tenant's needs.
- Lighting: LED lighting is common for energy efficiency and long lifespan. Motion sensors and daylight harvesting systems can further reduce energy consumption.
- Backup Systems: Industrial buildings may require backup generators or uninterruptible power supplies (UPS) for critical operations.
- Distribution: Ensure electrical panels and conduits are well-placed for expansion or upgrades. Redundant systems can add reliability.
- Specialized Systems: Considerations for EV charging stations, robotics, or automation systems may be necessary in modern facilities.

Plumbing

- Water Supply: Adequate water pressure and availability are essential, especially for manufacturing operations or fire suppression systems.
- Drainage: Interior drainage systems should handle spills and cleaning processes effectively, including sloped floors and trench drains where necessary. Furthermore, there should be separation or filtering spills of certain materials and liquids from emptying into main sewer system.
- Special Requirements: Certain industries (e.g., food processing, pharmaceuticals) may require stainless steel plumbing, grease traps, or specialized filtration systems.

Mechanical Systems

- HVAC: Heating, ventilation, and air conditioning systems must be tailored to the building's purpose. Warehousing requires different climate control than food processing facilities.
- Zoning: Multi-zone HVAC systems allow for better control of temperature in specific areas.
- Air Quality: High-efficiency filters and air exchange systems may be necessary for clean environments.
- Fire Suppression: Sprinkler systems are often mandatory. Types include wet, dry, or pre-action systems depending on the building's use. NFPA standards should guide design and implementation.
- Automation: Building management systems (BMS) can integrate HVAC, lighting, and security for improved efficiency and control.

Dock Equipment

- Doors: Roll-up or sectional doors should be properly sealed and sized for truck access. High-speed doors are ideal for temperature-controlled areas.
- Levelers and Seals: Dock levelers accommodate various truck sizes, while seals minimize air, pest, and water intrusion. Verify the capacity of levelers to handle loaded trailers.
- Bumpers and Guards: Dock bumpers protect the building's structure from truck impacts. See more in chapter 13: Loading.

Water Management

Handling water effectively is critical to protect the building and its surroundings.

Drainage Systems

- Interior: Ensure floor drains are placed strategically for cleaning or spills. Grated trench drains are common in manufacturing and food processing facilities.
- Exterior: Perimeter drainage systems, such as French drains, keep water away from the foundation. Check for adequate grading around the building.

Stormwater Management

- Storm Ponds: Detention and retention ponds manage excess runoff. Detention ponds temporarily hold water, while retention ponds permanently store it.
- Regulations: Compliance with local stormwater regulations is mandatory. Verify permits and environmental impact assessments.
- Grading: Proper grading ensures water flows away from the building. Slope percentages should align with local codes and best practices.

Land Upgrades

The land surrounding the building is often as important as the structure itself.

Paving

- Asphalt: Common for parking lots and light-duty areas. Maintenance includes sealing cracks and periodic resurfacing.
- Concrete: Preferred for heavy-duty truck courts due to its durability. Expansion joints and rebar reinforcement are critical for long-term performance.
- Gravel: A cost-effective option for areas with lower traffic. Proper compaction and grading are necessary to avoid ruts and erosion.

Landscaping

- Erosion Control: Landscaping minimizes soil erosion and enhances water absorption. Bioswales or rain gardens can further assist in stormwater management.
- Aesthetics: Trees and shrubs can improve curb appeal while providing shade. Consider low-maintenance, drought-resistant plants.

Fencing and Security

- Perimeter Fencing: Adds security and defines property

boundaries.

- Lighting: Well-placed exterior lighting deters vandalism and improves safety. LED floodlights with motion sensors are a common choice.
- Access Control: Automated gates, card readers, and surveillance systems enhance security.

Key Considerations

- Regulations: Be aware of zoning laws, building codes, and environmental regulations. Consult with experts to navigate complex compliance requirements.
- Futureproofing: Designing with flexibility for expansion or changes in use can increase a building's lifespan and marketability. Include Electrical infrastructure for future system expansion, modular spaces, and adaptable layouts.
- Tenant Needs: Align construction features with the needs of potential tenants, such as ceiling heights, dock configurations, or specific utility requirements.
- Resilience: Considerations for extreme weather, such as hurricanes, earthquakes, or heavy snowfall, may require reinforced structures or additional systems.

By focusing on these elements, you can evaluate the quality and suitability of an industrial property effectively, ensuring that it meets the demands of both present and future users.

Summary

Industrial construction is a complex process that demands careful planning, precise execution, and expert oversight. Involving professionals such as architects, engineers, and project managers ensures that every aspect of the project is handled with expertise. Their experience helps avoid costly mistakes, enhances safety, and delivers a property that meets both current and future needs. Whether you're building a new facility or retrofitting an existing one, having the right professionals on your team is an investment that pays off in quality and long-term value.

Thank you to Darin Brindle with Peak Built General Contracting for his assistance on this chapter. Connect with Darin at www.peakbuilt.ca

14

Loading

EFFICIENT LOADING AND UNLOADING operations are crucial to the success of industrial properties, directly impacting operational efficiency, tenant satisfaction, and property value. Thoughtful design of loading areas enhances logistics, reduces operational costs, and accommodates diverse tenant needs. This chapter explores the importance of loading operations, discusses the various types of loading doors, and provides insights into dock-level and grade-level loading options.

Types of Loading Doors

Loading doors, sometimes referred to as roll-up doors, facilitate the movement of goods in and out of industrial buildings. They are typically constructed from insulated metal or aluminum for durability and thermal efficiency. Upgraded options like polycarbonate or glass panels enhance aesthetics and allow natural light, improving workplace conditions and reducing lighting costs. Loading doors are generally categorized into dock-level and grade-level doors.

Dock-Level Loading Doors

Dock-level doors are specifically designed to align with the height of standard truck trailer beds (approximately 48 inches). They are essential for efficient loading and unloading of trucks and are common in distribution centers and logistics operations.

Figure 11: Dock loading

Dock loading doors are typically accompanied by dock levelers, which bridge height gaps between the dock and truck beds (ranging from 42–62 inches).

Manual Dock Levelers: Operated via pull-chain or lever, cost-effective for low-volume operations but require more labor.
Hydraulic Dock Levelers: Offer automated push-button operations, smoother transitions, higher weight capacities, and improved safety, ideal for high-volume facilities.

Figure 12: A dock leveller creating a bridge from the trailer to the warehouse floor.

Property Access and Truck Maneuverability

Smooth truck access is essential to loading efficiency:

- Verify that 53-foot semi-trucks can easily access the property from main highways without encountering obstacles such as sharp turns, low bridges, or narrow roads.
- Evaluate proximity to specialized access points like rail sidings, water ports, or intermodal yards for enhanced logistical capabilities.
- Design facilities to accommodate counterclockwise truck movement for better visibility and maneuverability. Recommended yard depth from dock face to yard edge is 130–135 feet, extending to 185–205 feet for shared yards.

Loading Area and Trailer Parking

Efficient design of the loading area is critical:

- Ensure apron spaces have at least 135 feet of depth for comfortable truck maneuvering.
- Allocate trailer parking stalls measuring 10 feet by 55 feet with an additional 65 feet of maneuvering space.
- Concrete aprons extending at least 60 feet from the dock face help prevent damage from frequent trailer movements.
- Wheel stops should be positioned 12 feet from the stall ends, with concrete landing pads extending 40–60 feet for versatility.

Cross-Docking Operations

Cross-docking is a logistics strategy where incoming goods are immediately sorted and directly transferred from inbound trucks to outbound vehicles, reducing or eliminating the need for storage. This practice significantly enhances operational efficiency, reduces handling costs, and accelerates product movement:

Layout and Design: Cross-dock facilities typically feature loading doors on two opposite sides, allowing goods to flow quickly from receiving to shipping without prolonged storage.

Operational Efficiency: Minimizes inventory holding costs, improves inventory turnover, and streamlines supply chain processes.

Ideal for High-Volume Facilities: Commonly used by retail distribution centers, express delivery companies, and third-party logistics providers managing large volumes of perishable or time-sensitive goods.

Facility Requirements: Efficient cross-docking requires ample dock doors, sufficient apron space for vehicle maneuvering, and well-designed staging areas for rapid sorting and redistribution of goods.

Grade-Level Loading Doors

Grade-level doors provide direct, ground-level access to buildings, critical for operations involving heavy equipment, machinery, or frequent vehicular entry. Common in manufacturing facilities, flex buildings, and smaller warehouse operations. Standard door sizes typically range from 12 feet wide by 14–16 feet high, with larger sizes available for specialized applications. Adequate clearance around doors ensures smooth vehicle entry and exit, reducing operational delays.

User-Specific Loading Requirements

Different tenants have varied operational needs impacting their loading requirements:

Limited Loading Needs: Smaller businesses or those handling lighter, less frequent shipments typically prefer minimal infrastructure, often satisfied with grade-level doors.

High-Volume Operations: Distribution centers or fulfillment warehouses require numerous dock-level doors to support simultaneous loading and unloading, enhancing throughput efficiency.

Combined Dock and Grade-Level Loading: Businesses such as manufacturers or equipment rental companies benefit from having both dock-level and grade-level access, providing operational flexibility.

Specialized Loading Options

Certain properties benefit from specialized loading capabilities:

Rail-Side Loading: Direct rail access facilitates efficient logistics for heavy or bulk cargo, requiring specialized docks and sufficient yard space for railcar handling.

Water-Side Loading: Properties near waterways or ports benefit from docks designed for barge or ship loading, significantly reducing transportation costs for heavy or international freight.

Solutions for Limited Access and Loading Constraints

If a property lacks adequate access for semi-trucks or doesn't have the preferred type of loading doors, several solutions can enhance functionality:

- Adjust Loading Methods: Use forklifts or pallet jacks to transfer goods from larger trucks parked outside the immediate loading area to smaller vehicles or through smaller doors.
- Portable Dock Ramps: Temporary dock ramps can bridge the height gap between trucks and buildings without permanent dock installations, offering flexibility for grade-level doors.
- Door Modifications: Retrofitting existing loading doors or installing new doors (e.g., converting a grade-level door to a dock-level door) can significantly enhance loading capabilities.
- External Loading Platforms: Building external loading docks or ramps can improve functionality without major structural modifications to the existing facility.

Loading Technology and Future Trends

Facilities should anticipate evolving logistics trends:

- Prepare infrastructure for autonomous or electric trucks.
- Include adequate staging areas near docks for efficient operations.
- Use CAD and simulation tools to optimize yard layouts and truck maneuverability.

Case Study: Optimizing a Multi-Tenant Industrial Facility

A recent 150,000-square-foot industrial development effectively accommodated diverse tenant needs through:

- A balanced combination of 15 dock-level doors and 5 grade-level doors.
- Cross-docking layouts facilitating rapid movement of goods.

- Reinforced concrete apron space for heavy-duty truck operations.

This flexible design attracted both logistics providers requiring efficient dock-level loading and manufacturers needing grade-level access, enhancing the property's marketability and operational efficiency.

Key Rules of Thumb:

Truck drive width: Minimum 40 feet with a 40-foot inside curb radius.
Yard depth: 130–135 feet standard; 185–205 feet for shared yards.
Standard dock height: 48 inches.
Trailer stalls: 10 feet by 55 feet with 65 feet of maneuvering space.
Concrete landing pads: Extend 40–60 feet from trailer parking areas.

By considering these factors, industrial properties can maximize operational efficiency, tenant satisfaction, and overall market competitiveness.

15

Ceiling Heights

CEILING HEIGHTS SIGNIFICANTLY impact the functionality, marketability, and overall value of industrial properties. While it might appear to be a straightforward measurement, understanding the nuances between physical height and clear ceiling height is essential for accurate property assessment and future planning.

Physical Height vs. Clear Ceiling Height

Physical Height: Refers to the total interior height of a building, measured from the floor to the underside of the roof deck.
Clear Ceiling Height: The usable vertical space, measured from the floor to the lowest structural element, such as beams or trusses. Clear ceiling height is the critical metric tenants evaluate when determining the usability of industrial spaces.

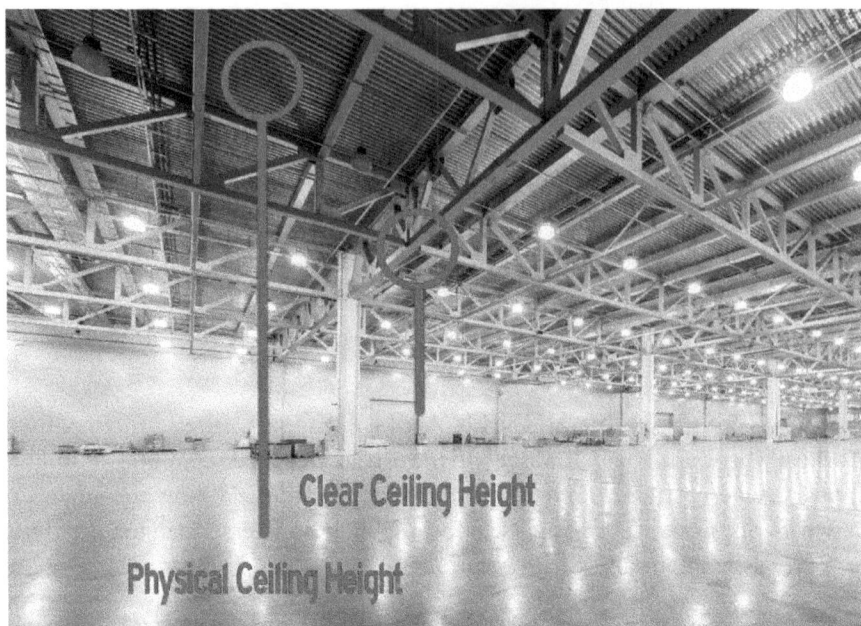

Figure 13: Clear Ceiling Height vs Physical Ceiling Height

Evolution of Ceiling Heights

Ceiling heights in industrial buildings have progressively increased over recent decades, primarily driven by:

Advances in Forklift Technology: Modern forklifts operate efficiently at higher levels.
Enhanced Racking Systems: Allow optimal use of vertical storage space.
Improved Fire Suppression: Modern sprinkler systems safely accommodate higher storage racks.

Historically, industrial buildings featured clear heights of approximately 14–20 feet, whereas contemporary facilities typically offer 24–40 feet or more.

Ceiling Heights in Flat vs. Pitched Roofs

Industrial properties usually have either flat or pitched roofs:

Flat Roofs: Offer uniform height throughout, maximizing storage consistency and space utilization.

Pitched Roofs: Feature varying heights, from lower eave heights along walls to higher peak heights at the center. This design influences storage configurations and operational efficiency.

Why Ceiling Heights Matter

Ceiling heights affect several key aspects:

Storage Capacity: Higher ceilings significantly increase cubic storage volume, essential for logistics and warehousing operations.

Operational Flexibility: Greater vertical clearance supports diverse operational needs, including the movement of large equipment or installation of high racking systems.

Tenant Appeal: Properties with higher ceilings attract a broader range of tenants and can command higher market values. Conversely, lower ceilings might limit the property's versatility, narrowing potential user groups.

Real-World Examples of Ceiling Height Usage

Modern Logistics Warehouses: Typically constructed with clear heights of 36–40 feet to maximize efficient vertical racking and automated systems.

Specialized Facilities: Certain applications, like aircraft hangars or industrial production plants, may require significantly higher ceilings, such as NASA's Vehicle Assembly Building, which reaches 526 feet.

Older Industrial Facilities: Buildings predating modern logistics standards often feature lower ceilings (under 20 feet) suitable for specific uses like small-scale manufacturing, automotive repair, or workshops.

Key Factors in Evaluating Ceiling Heights

When considering ceiling heights, evaluate tenant requirements and potential future uses:

Tenant Operations: Distribution centers prioritize higher ceilings for high-density storage; manufacturers may require high ceilings for machinery clearance.

Futureproofing: Higher ceilings provide flexibility, minimizing the risk of obsolescence and accommodating evolving industrial practices.

Cost Implications: Higher ceilings can elevate construction costs due to increased materials, structural support, and heating or cooling expenses. Balancing initial investment against long-term flexibility is essential.

Case Study: The Importance of Ceiling Height Planning

An owner of a safety training company constructed a high-quality industrial facility with premium finishes, expecting long-term personal use. Given that his business didn't require significant vertical space, he chose a ceiling height of only 14 feet to reduce initial and ongoing costs.

After unexpectedly selling his company, the facility became vacant. Despite the building's excellent quality, it faced significant leasing and resale challenges because of its limited ceiling height. The owner had to make multiple price reductions to attract suitable buyers. Although profitable overall due to the business sale, this example underscores the critical importance of ceiling height in planning and its direct impact on future marketability.

Summary

Ceiling heights are a pivotal component of industrial real estate, influencing operational capability, tenant appeal, and property valuation. As industries evolve, the trend toward higher clear ceiling heights continues, making it an essential consideration for both property evaluation and new developments. Understanding and balancing tenant needs, future flexibility, and cost implications are crucial to optimizing industrial real estate investments.

16

Column Grids

COLUMN GRIDS dictate the structural layout of a building, directly influencing functionality, storage efficiency, and construction costs. A column grid refers to the systematic arrangement of vertical support columns within a building, typically following a uniform pattern to optimize load distribution and maximize usable space.

Importance of Column Spacing

Column spacing significantly impacts a building's layout, storage capabilities, and adaptability. Efficient column grids maximize operational flow and accommodate specific industrial needs, from warehousing to manufacturing and recreational uses.

Standard Column Grid Configurations

Typical industrial column grid spacings range from 25' x 50' to 50' x 50', depending on factors like building size, load requirements, and intended usage. Older buildings often have tighter grids, while newer distribution centers frequently adopt larger grids—up to 60' x 60' or greater—to maximize operational flexibility and accommodate advanced racking systems.

Figure 14: A warehouse with internal columns

Key factors influencing column spacing include:

- Building height and structural load requirements
- Racking layouts and aisle widths
- Material handling equipment such as forklifts and conveyors
- Land availability and construction budget

Clear Span Design

Clear span refers to structural designs that eliminate internal support columns, providing uninterrupted open spaces. This layout is highly desirable for maximizing storage flexibility, maneuverability, and operational efficiency.

Advantages of clear span design include:

- Unobstructed space ideal for high-density storage and complex racking systems
- Enhanced maneuverability for forklifts, cranes, and automated guided vehicles (AGVs)
- Greater adaptability for multiple industrial and commercial uses
- Particularly beneficial for indoor recreation facilities

Figure 15: An example of a clear span building.

Ceiling Heights

Unlike flat roofs, a roofing system with extensive clear spans often incorporates a pitched or gable style system. You might hear it called a Butler style roofing system (which is a nod to Butler Manufacturing who has been making pre-engineered metal building systems specifically designed to span long distances without interior columns). Butler style roofs will have two important measurements to note:

Height at the peak (highest point of the roof);
Height at the eave (lowest point of the roof).

Similar to any other type of use you'll want to take the measurement to the underside of any structural element (ie/ truss or beam).

Figure 16: Peak height vs Eave Height.

Cost vs. Functionality Considerations

While clear span structures offer unparalleled space efficiency, they require more robust structural support systems, increasing construction costs. Traditional column grids represent a more economical alternative but can restrict operational flexibility due to interior obstructions.

Design Factor	Standard Column Grid	Clear Span
Cost	Lower construction costs	Higher due to reinforced trusses and materials
Space Utilization	Limited by interior columns	Maximum efficiency with uninterrupted open space
Flexibility	May require column workarounds in racking layouts	Fully adaptable for different warehouse functions
Construction Complexity	Easier and faster to construct	Requires advanced engineering and larger supports

Rising Demand for Clear Span in Indoor Recreation

Indoor recreation venues, such as sports facilities, trampoline parks, and event centers, increasingly prefer clear span designs to maximize usable floor space without interference from structural columns. Many industrial properties with clear span configurations are being repurposed for these recreational activities.

Important considerations for indoor recreation adaptations include:

Insurance Risks: Higher liability risks from injuries and large gatherings can lead to increased insurance premiums. Comprehensive liability and property coverage, along with adherence to safety regulations, are crucial.

Zoning & Permitting: Recreation uses may require special zoning approvals or conditional permits. Compliance with local building codes, parking regulations, and occupancy standards must be thoroughly evaluated.

Impact on Tenants: Recreation tenants typically generate high parking demand, potentially disrupting other tenants' operations. Careful property and parking lot management is necessary to maintain harmony among mixed-use tenants.

Building Wear and Tear: High visitor traffic significantly increases wear and tear on floors, walls, restrooms, and HVAC systems, necessitating higher maintenance and possibly reinforced infrastructure.

Engineering Considerations for Clear Span Structures

Clear span designs introduce unique engineering challenges due to their larger open spaces:

Load Distribution: Without internal columns, roofs and exterior walls must handle higher wind, snow, and operational loads, requiring reinforced trusses and bracing.

Material Selection: Durable materials such as steel, laminated timber, or space frame systems are essential to sustain structural integrity.

Enhanced Foundations: Clear span buildings may require stronger foundations to efficiently transfer and manage increased structural loads.

Futureproofing with Clear Span Designs

Clear span buildings offer greater adaptability for future technological advancements and changing tenant needs. The rise of automation, robotics, and mixed-use industrial parks underscores the growing demand for column-free spaces that accommodate automated systems and flexible configurations.

Summary

Choosing between traditional column grids and clear span designs depends on specific operational goals, budget constraints, and long-term adaptability. Clear span structures provide maximum flexibility but at higher construction costs, while conventional grids offer cost efficiency but limit layout options. Ultimately, collaborating early with structural engineers and warehouse designers ensures alignment of column grid choices with current operational demands and future business growth.

17

Site Coverage Ratio

THE SITE COVERAGE RATIO (SCR), also referred to as the property coverage ratio or building coverage ratio, is a vital metric in industrial real estate. It measures how much of a parcel of land is covered by buildings or structures. Beyond being a key tool for developers and planners, it's an essential consideration for companies looking to determine the availability of excess land for future use.

Definition and Calculation

The site coverage ratio represents the percentage of a property's total land area that is covered by buildings at ground level. It is calculated using the following formula:

$$\text{Site Coverage Ratio} = \left(\frac{\text{Building Size}}{\text{Total Land Area}} \right) \times 100$$

Where:
Building Size: The total ground-level area covered by all buildings on the site (referenced in Chapter 10: Measurements).
Total Land Area: The entire area of the parcel of land.

Example:

If an industrial property has a building size of 50,000 square feet on a 100,000 square foot parcel of land, the site coverage ratio would be:

$$\text{Site Coverage Ratio} = \left(\frac{50{,}000}{100{,}000} \right) \times 100 = 50\%$$

This indicates that 50% of the land area is covered by the building.

Depending on local zoning regulations, this ratio may be acceptable or could exceed limits, impacting the usability and development potential of the property.

Importance in Industrial Real Estate

- Zoning Regulations: Many municipalities have zoning requirements that specify the maximum allowable site coverage ratio. These rules help control building density, manage urban sprawl, and ensure sufficient open spaces.
- Infrastructure Planning: Properties with higher site coverage ratios often have less room for critical features like parking, loading areas, or green spaces. This can affect traffic flow, operational efficiency, and environmental considerations.
- Valuation and Development Potential: The site coverage ratio influences a property's value and development feasibility. Properties with low site coverage ratios often have additional land available for future expansion or development, making them more attractive to investors and developers.

Applications in Industrial Properties

Manufacturing and IOS Properties: The site coverage ratio is most often referenced for manufacturing and industrial outdoor storage (IOS) properties, where land availability for yards, equipment, or vehicle storage is critical.

Warehouses and Flex Properties: While less commonly emphasized for warehouses or flex properties compared to manufacturing or IOS, the SCR is still important.

For warehouses, the SCR can influence the efficiency of truck maneuverability, dock access, and the adequacy of staging areas. Additionally, properties with lower SCR can accommodate larger truck courts, additional trailer storage, or future expansion.

For flex properties, a lower SCR may provide opportunities for extra parking, outdoor storage, or enhanced landscaping, which can significantly increase tenant appeal and property versatility.

Low Site Coverage Ratios and IOS

As discussed in Chapter 6: Industrial Outdoor Storage, properties with low site coverage ratios are often classified as IOS. These properties typically prioritize yard space over building area, allowing for the storage of vehicles, equipment, or materials. For example, an IOS property with only 10% of its land covered by buildings might dedicate the remaining 90% to open yard storage.

The Trend of Higher Coverage Ratios

In urban areas with high land costs, developers often push for higher site coverage ratios to maximize the building footprint and improve financial returns. However, this approach can lead to challenges, such as reduced space for parking and truck maneuverability, as well as potential conflicts with zoning requirements.

Summary

The site coverage ratio is a crucial metric for understanding and optimizing land use in industrial real estate. By calculating the proportion of land covered by buildings, developers, investors, and planners can evaluate a property's functionality, compliance with zoning regulations, and potential for future development. Whether assessing a manufacturing facility, an IOS property, or a warehouse, understanding the site coverage ratio ensures informed decision-making and strategic planning for industrial real estate projects.

18

Electrical

ELECTRICITY is a fundamental yet often misunderstood element of industrial real estate. It powers essential operations—from machinery and lighting to advanced technological systems—making it critical for property owners, developers, and tenants alike to understand electrical infrastructure thoroughly. This chapter covers the foundational concepts, practical considerations, and important factors in evaluating and enhancing electrical capacity in industrial buildings.

Understanding Electrical Basics

Understanding electrical systems is essential—especially when considering power requirements, which can vary dramatically based on the type of industrial use. Some operations, particularly manufacturing and heavy-powered industrial facilities, require substantial electrical capacity.

Just how much power might you need? Well, consider the iconic disbelief of Doc Brown from *Back to the Future*:

"1.21 gigawatts?! 1.21 gigawatts?! Great Scott!"

While 1.21 gigawatts (or 1,210 megawatts) would indeed be extreme for even the most power-hungry facility, Doc's famous astonishment humorously emphasizes an important point: underestimating power requirements can seriously impact operations. Careful planning ensures facilities have ample electrical infrastructure to avoid costly surprises or operational delays.

Electricity involves several key terms:

Amperage (Amps): Represents the current or flow of electrons through a circuit. Higher amperage indicates greater electrical capacity.
Voltage (Volts): The electrical "pressure" pushing current through a circuit. Higher voltage levels allow for more efficient transmission of power.
Power (Watts): Calculated as volts multiplied by amps (Volts x Amps = Watts). This measurement indicates the actual electrical work performed, such as running equipment or illuminating spaces.
Volt-Amperes (VA): Reflect apparent power, considering system efficiency. Typically relevant in specialized contexts, managed primarily by electrical professionals.

Single Phase vs. Three Phase Power

Industrial buildings predominantly use **Alternating Current (AC)**, available in single-phase or three-phase systems:

Single Phase: Suitable for residential or small commercial uses, offering limited capacity and intermittent current flow.
Three Phase: Common in industrial settings, providing continuous current through three overlapping waveforms, crucial for heavy machinery and continuous operation.

Confirming the presence of three-phase power is essential during property evaluations. Retrofitting from single-phase to three-phase is expensive and complex, requiring substantial upgrades to transformers and utility connections.

Common Voltage Standards

Voltage standards typically vary by country:

United States: 480 volts is standard for industrial properties.
Canada: 600 volts is commonly used.
Precise voltage levels can differ between buildings based on their specific electrical configurations, so verification with local utilities is necessary.

The Role of Transformers

Transformers adjust voltage to meet specific operational needs:

Step-Up Transformers: Increase voltage to support large equipment or heavy machinery.

Step-Down Transformers: Reduce voltage for standard lighting, HVAC systems, and office equipment.

Correct sizing and selection (measured in kVA) of transformers is crucial to prevent system inefficiencies or equipment damage.

Figure 17: An electrical room with multiple transformers

Demand Charges and Utility Contracts

High-power users typically negotiate utility contracts incorporating demand charges. These charges are based on the peak electricity usage recorded during specific billing periods. Contracted minimum demands may apply regardless of actual usage, potentially impacting operating costs even if a facility is vacant. Landlords and tenants must carefully forecast energy needs to negotiate suitable agreements and avoid unnecessary financial burdens.

Practical Considerations for Industrial Properties

Assessing Existing Power

- Verify available amperage and voltage.
- Confirm three-phase capability and transformer specifications.

- Evaluate historical usage and current demand levels through utility bills and professional inspections.

Upgrading Power Infrastructure

Expanding power capacity can be constrained by:

- Existing grid limitations and infrastructure capacity.
- Rising regional power demands impacting availability.
- High costs and lengthy permitting processes associated with infrastructure upgrades.

Attracting Suitable Tenants

Properties with inadequate power infrastructure may struggle to attract tenants, particularly in manufacturing or advanced technology sectors. Understanding regional standards and proactively enhancing electrical infrastructure can significantly improve tenant appeal and property value.

Equipment and Operational Power Requirements

Tenants must calculate peak and average power needs, accounting for simultaneous vs. intermittent operation of machinery and systems.
Facilities with energy-intensive operations like data centers or manufacturing plants must ensure robust electrical systems capable of supporting peak demands reliably.

Professional Expertise and Support

Electrical infrastructure demands specialized knowledge. Engaging professional support is crucial:

Electricians: Conduct accurate power assessments, verify compliance, and perform essential upgrades.
Electrical Engineers: Design customized, scalable electrical solutions that align with operational needs, regulatory requirements, and long-term planning.

Their expertise ensures that the facility's electrical system supports current operations and future expansions effectively.

Case Study #1: Power Upgrades for Tenant Attraction

An industrial park initially constructed with standard 400-amp, three-phase service struggled to attract technology-driven tenants requiring substantial electrical capacity. After assessing market demand, the owner invested in upgrading to an 800-amp system with additional transformers and distribution infrastructure. This enhancement attracted tenants from industries such as robotics manufacturing and biotechnology, increasing occupancy rates, lease values, and long-term property competitiveness.

Case Study #2: Electrical Risks in Industrial Real Estate

An industrial tenant purchased a highly specialized welding machine from France. This sophisticated piece of equipment was hyper-sensitive to voltage fluctuations. Shortly after installation, the tenant experienced significant electrical downtime.

Upon investigation, it became clear the root of the issue wasn't internal, but rather external. A large book-binding company located approximately half a mile away was using massive printing presses. Whenever these machines activated, they caused substantial voltage drops throughout the local grid, leading to the welding machine repeatedly failing and requiring frequent restarts.

To address the issue, the tenant had to invest in specialized electrical equipment designed to stabilize voltage fluctuations. Additionally, they learned a critical lesson about assessing the power infrastructure and understanding neighborhood dynamics.

Lessons Learned:

Know Your Neighbors: If power is fundamental to business operations, evaluate neighboring industrial operations as their electrical demands can significantly impact your own power stability.

Infrastructure Risks: Large industrial equipment can offer high profitability, but also carries significant operational and financial risks. Voltage fluctuations illustrate the razor's edge between profit and loss.

Stress Testing and Integrity: Proper stress-testing of electrical and structural systems is vital. A single oversight, like drilling a hole in stress-tested panels, can compromise the entire system's integrity.

Roof Load Considerations: Older industrial buildings often weren't designed for modern installations, such as solar panels, leading to additional structural risks.

Power Priority: Understand your position in the local power distribution hierarchy. Power allocation and prioritization can significantly impact operational reliability.

Ultimately, this case underscores that managing electrical systems in industrial real estate is a complex but crucial element of successful operations. Electricity itself can be inherently risky, as unforeseen circumstances—such as a new company moving into the neighborhood with significant power demands—can unexpectedly alter power availability and stability, creating additional operational risks.

Expert Insight

"Don't take the subject of power lightly, because if you overlook one critical component—either as a company occupying the space or as a property owner— you might have insufficient power for your needs. It's incumbent upon tenants and landlords to get ahead of this as quickly as possible."
—Bryce Pasiuk, Electrical Engineer

Summary

Electricity significantly influences the value, functionality, and marketability of industrial properties. Understanding key electrical concepts, carefully assessing infrastructure needs, managing utility contracts, and leveraging professional expertise help property owners and tenants ensure electrical systems meet both current operational demands and future growth requirements.

19

Lighting

LIGHTING HAS EVOLVED significantly over the years to meet the changing demands of energy efficiency, worker productivity, and operational needs. This chapter explores the historical and modern methods of industrial lighting, emerging technologies, critical considerations for lighting in industrial properties, recommended lighting levels, and regulatory considerations.

Historical Lighting Methods

Skylights: Historically, warehouses relied heavily on natural light during the day, using skylights and large windows to maximize daylight exposure. While cost-effective, this method was limited by weather conditions and time of day.
Incandescent Lighting: Among the first electric lighting solutions, incandescent bulbs provided warm light but were highly inefficient, consuming significant energy and producing excessive heat.

Modern Lighting Methods

Light Emitting Diode (LED) Lighting:

Currently the most popular choice for industrial lighting due to their high energy efficiency, long lifespan, and ability to provide bright, clear light.

Advantages: Versatile, with various color temperatures to suit different needs. Compatible with smart controls and sensors for optimized energy use. Reduce maintenance costs and enhance workplace safety with consistent illumination.
Applications: Widely used in warehouses, manufacturing facilities, and

outdoor areas.

Fluorescent Lighting:

T12, T8, and T5 Lamps: Fluorescent lighting became popular in the mid-20th century for its efficiency compared to incandescent bulbs. T5 lamps are the most energy-efficient and compact of the three options.

Advantages: Bright illumination, relatively low heat output, and cost-effective operation.
Applications: Commonly used in warehouses and industrial spaces requiring consistent light over large areas.

High-Intensity Discharge (HID) Lighting:

Metal Halide: Produces bright, white light suitable for high-ceiling warehouses. However, these lamps take time to warm up and are less energy-efficient compared to newer technologies.
High-Pressure Sodium: Known for long life and efficiency but emit a yellowish light, which may not be ideal for all applications.
Mercury Vapor: Once popular for their bluish light, these are now largely phased out due to inefficiency and environmental concerns.

Induction Lighting:

Similar to fluorescent lighting but without electrodes, making these lights more durable and long-lasting. Used in situations requiring reliable, long-term lighting, such as high-usage areas.

Compact Fluorescent Lamps (CFLs):

Smaller versions of standard fluorescent lamps, offering better energy efficiency than incandescent bulbs. Often used in smaller industrial spaces or areas with space constraints.

Emerging Lighting Technologies

Sensors and Automation: Incorporate motion or occupancy sensors to adjust lighting based on activity and daylight availability, further enhancing energy efficiency.

IoT Integration: Lighting systems connected to the Internet of Things (IoT) allow remote control, monitoring, and data collection for optimizing energy usage.

Recommended Lighting Levels

Industrial lighting standards vary depending on the tasks performed:

Warehousing: Typically, 20-30 foot-candles (200-300 lux).
Manufacturing and Assembly: Generally requires higher illumination, around 50-75 foot-candles (500-750 lux).
Precision Tasks (inspection or fine assembly): May require 100+ foot-candles (1000+ lux).

Color Temperature Explained

Color temperature, measured in Kelvin (K), indicates the appearance of light:

Warm White (2700-3500K): Creates a comfortable, relaxing atmosphere, suitable for break rooms or administrative areas.
Neutral White (4000-4500K): Balanced lighting that reduces eye strain, ideal for general warehouse or manufacturing areas.
Cool White/Daylight (5000-6500K): Enhances visibility and concentration, recommended for precision tasks and detailed inspections.

Cost-Benefit Analysis of LED Upgrades

Upgrading from traditional fluorescent or HID lighting to LED lighting can result in energy savings of up to 50-75%. LEDs also significantly reduce maintenance costs due to their longer lifespan, providing a typical return on investment within 1-3 years depending on usage and electricity rates.

Regulatory and Environmental Compliance

Regulatory requirements increasingly favor energy-efficient lighting. Many jurisdictions offer rebates or incentives for LED upgrades. Property owners should also ensure compliance with local energy codes, environmental standards, and lighting quality guidelines to avoid fines or operational disruptions.

Emergency Lighting

Industrial facilities require emergency lighting and clearly marked exit signs powered by battery backups to ensure occupant safety during power outages or emergencies. Compliance with local safety codes (e.g., NFPA 101 or OSHA standards) is mandatory to provide adequate illumination for safe evacuation.

Key Considerations for Industrial Lighting

Fixture selection may be based on area usage (potential for impact, corrosion resistance, wet or moisture-resistant ratings).

- Warehouse Layout: Ceiling height, racking systems, and open spaces impact the type and placement of lighting fixtures.
- Energy Efficiency: Energy-efficient lighting, such as LEDs or smart systems, can significantly reduce operational costs.
- Worker Productivity and Safety: Bright, consistent lighting reduces eye strain and improves visibility, enhancing both productivity and safety.
- Maintenance Requirements: Longer-lasting systems like LEDs or induction lighting reduce maintenance frequency and costs.
- Light Quality: Choose lighting with appropriate color temperature and brightness for the intended purpose.

Summary

Industrial lighting has evolved from natural lighting to advanced LED and smart systems. Each method offers distinct advantages suitable for specific applications. By understanding lighting options and considering factors like worker safety, maintenance, energy savings, and regulatory compliance, property owners and tenants can implement solutions that enhance productivity and reduce costs.

20

HVAC (Heating, Ventilation, and Air Conditioning)

HEATING, VENTILATION, AND AIR CONDITIONING (HVAC) systems regulate temperature, humidity, and air quality, creating safe, comfortable, and efficient working environments. Effective HVAC systems enhance employee comfort and support industrial processes by managing contaminants like dust, fumes, and emissions. This chapter covers the purpose, types, key components, design considerations, maintenance practices, specialized solutions, critical trends in industrial HVAC systems, and includes a practical case study.

Purpose and Importance

HVAC systems in industrial settings maintain consistent indoor conditions by controlling temperature, humidity, and ventilation. Proper climate control ensures optimal working conditions and protects sensitive processes or products. Effective ventilation removes pollutants, maintaining air quality and regulatory compliance. Well-designed HVAC systems also significantly enhance energy efficiency, reducing operating costs.

Types of HVAC Systems

Rooftop units (RTUs) are common in industrial facilities, efficiently managing heating, cooling, and ventilation while preserving valuable indoor space. Forced-air furnaces and overhead gas-fired units provide practical heating solutions for warehouses and smaller facilities. Radiant heating is effective in large, open spaces, directly warming people and objects rather than air.

Larger facilities might use chillers and boilers for centralized cooling and heating. Make-Up Air Units (MAUs) provide critical fresh air replacement in buildings with high ventilation demands. Variable Air Volume (VAV) and Direct Expansion (DX) systems offer tailored solutions for flexible, efficient climate control.

Key Components

Essential HVAC components include Air Handling Units (AHUs) that distribute conditioned air, well-sealed and insulated ductwork, and filters that remove particulates for indoor air quality. Thermostats and centralized controls allow precise system management, often integrated with Building Management Systems (BMS) for comprehensive monitoring. Fans and ventilators circulate air, especially in areas generating heat or emissions.

Air Conditioning for Office and Flex Spaces

Office and flex spaces within industrial facilities typically require dedicated air conditioning systems to maintain comfortable working conditions. The general rule of thumb for sizing office air conditioning is about 1 ton of cooling per 300–400 square feet of office space, depending on building insulation, window exposure, occupancy levels, and local climate conditions. Properly sized air conditioning units not only maintain employee comfort but also enhance productivity by reducing fatigue and heat stress.

Occasionally, entire industrial facilities, such as manufacturing plants, distribution centers, or data centers, require full air conditioning. While this can provide significant operational advantages, it also involves considerable upfront investment in HVAC equipment and substantial ongoing operational costs. Cooling large cubic footage can dramatically increase energy expenses, making energy-efficient systems and strategic cooling management essential for controlling costs.

Humidity Control and Dehumidification

Managing humidity is critical in industrial environments, particularly in facilities handling sensitive products like electronics, pharmaceuticals, or food. Excess humidity can damage products, foster mold growth, and affect worker comfort. Technologies like desiccant dehumidifiers and dedicated humidity control units ensure optimal humidity levels, protecting product integrity and ensuring regulatory compliance.

Redundancy and Backup Systems

Reliable HVAC operations often require redundancy or backup systems to prevent costly downtime. Facilities may implement backup generators, redundant chillers, or multiple heating and cooling units to ensure uninterrupted HVAC performance during equipment failures or maintenance periods. Proper redundancy planning safeguards productivity and ensures continuous compliance with safety standards.

Indoor Air Quality (IAQ) Standards and Regulations

HVAC systems must adhere to established IAQ standards, including ASHRAE guidelines and OSHA regulations, to ensure healthy working conditions. Maintaining compliance involves controlling airborne contaminants, ensuring proper ventilation rates, and regularly testing air quality. Proper filtration, ventilation, and humidity control are essential in meeting these regulatory standards.

Lifecycle Cost Analysis

Evaluating HVAC systems requires lifecycle cost analysis, considering initial investment alongside ongoing operational, maintenance, and energy expenses. Systems with higher upfront costs may offer substantial savings over their lifespan through reduced energy use, lower maintenance requirements, and fewer repairs. Lifecycle cost analysis ensures long-term financial efficiency and informed decision-making.

Specialized HVAC Solutions

Certain industries demand specialized HVAC systems tailored to unique requirements. Cleanrooms require precise humidity, temperature, and particulate control. Cold storage warehouses rely on advanced refrigeration systems maintaining consistently low temperatures. Pharmaceutical manufacturing facilities demand stringent climate control to protect product quality. Data centers require intensive cooling solutions to manage substantial heat generated by equipment. Understanding and implementing these specialized solutions is crucial for specific industrial operations.

Design Considerations

Efficient HVAC design involves accurate load calculations, appropriate zoning for independent climate control, and specialized ventilation for facilities handling unique contaminants. High-efficiency systems with superior SEER ratings and heat recovery features significantly reduce operational costs.

Maintenance and Upkeep

Routine inspections, timely filter replacements, and proactive system monitoring extend HVAC system longevity, ensuring continuous efficiency and reliability. Regular maintenance identifies performance issues early, reducing downtime and operational disruptions.

Challenges and Trends

HVAC systems must address challenges like space constraints, high energy usage, and regulatory compliance. Integrating large HVAC equipment can be challenging, particularly in older facilities. Energy-efficient practices remain critical due to HVAC's significant operational costs.
Emerging trends include smart HVAC systems with automation and IoT technology for enhanced efficiency and control. Alternative energy sources, like solar-assisted heating and eco-friendly refrigerants, are becoming essential for meeting sustainability goals. Advanced filtration technologies, such as UV-C lights and HEPA filters, further improve indoor air quality.

Make-Up Air Units (MAUs)

Make-Up Air Units (MAUs) replenish indoor air exhausted by ventilation systems, maintaining air quality and pressure balance. Essential in facilities with significant exhaust needs, MAUs introduce fresh, conditioned air, preventing negative pressure and HVAC inefficiencies. Municipalities often mandate MAUs based on operational needs, exhaust rates, and occupancy levels. Installation involves careful planning for airflow, heating needs, and effective air distribution. Costs vary widely based on system complexity and features.

Case Study: Retrofit of HVAC in a Manufacturing Facility

A 75,000-square-foot manufacturing facility specializing in automotive components faced operational issues due to inadequate HVAC performance. High humidity and inconsistent temperatures were affecting product quality and employee productivity. The existing rooftop units (RTUs) were aging and unable to meet the facility's demanding climate control needs.

A comprehensive retrofit was undertaken, including the installation of high-efficiency RTUs, advanced humidity control systems, and a dedicated Make-Up Air Unit (MAU). The upgraded system significantly improved indoor air quality and reduced humidity fluctuations. After implementation, the facility reported a 20% increase in productivity, a 30% reduction in HVAC-related energy costs, and enhanced employee comfort. The retrofit also brought the facility into compliance with local air quality regulations, demonstrating the tangible benefits of strategic HVAC investments.

Summary

Efficient HVAC systems significantly impact industrial property operations, enhancing comfort, supporting processes, and ensuring regulatory compliance. Comprehensive understanding of system types, components, lifecycle costs, specialized solutions, and real-world applications allows property owners and tenants to optimize HVAC performance, manage costs effectively, and maintain long-term operational success.

21

Roofs

NOTHING KILLS MORE DEALS than issues with the roof. Alongside parking lots, roofs are among the most expensive components of a building to replace or repair, and their condition can significantly impact a transaction. Beyond the cost, roof replacements are disruptive and time-consuming, making them a critical consideration for industrial real estate owners and tenants alike.

A poorly maintained or aging roof can jeopardize lease negotiations, stall acquisitions, and increase operating costs. Whether evaluating an investment property, negotiating lease terms, or planning capital expenditures, understanding roofing types, maintenance requirements, and potential risks is essential.

Characteristics of Flat Roofs

Most industrial buildings feature flat roofs, in contrast to the sloped or pitched roofs commonly seen in residential properties. While they may appear entirely level, flat roofs are engineered with a slight slope (typically ¼ inch per foot) to facilitate drainage.

Advantages of Flat Roofs

- Space Utilization – Ideal for housing HVAC units, solar panels, skylights, and even green roofing systems, maximizing usable space.
- Ease of Maintenance and Repairs – Flat surfaces provide safer, easier access for inspections, maintenance, and repairs.
- Cost-Effectiveness – Requires fewer materials and simpler construction than sloped roofs, reducing installation costs.
- Structural Load Efficiency – Can support heavy mechanical

equipment when properly reinforced.

Challenges of Flat Roofs

- Drainage Issues – Poorly maintained drains lead to water pooling, accelerating membrane degradation and increasing leak risks.
- Shorter Lifespan – Some flat roofing systems, such as TPO or EPDM, may have shorter lifespans than metal or sloped roofing options.
- Higher Heat Absorption – Dark-colored flat roofs can trap heat, increasing cooling costs unless reflective coatings or white roofing membranes are used.

Types of Roofing Systems

The right roofing system depends on budget, climate, building use, and maintenance expectations. Below are the most common industrial roofing options:

Built-Up Roofing (BUR) – "Tar and Gravel"

A time-tested system made of multiple layers of bitumen (asphalt or tar) and reinforcing fabrics, known as "plys." This type of roof is durable and long-lasting. With proper maintenance a roof can last 20-30 years.

The system is both water and fire resistant as the gravel protects against UV exposure and fire hazards. This type of system requires strong structural support however and is a labor-intensive and costly installation.

Modified Bitumen Roofing – Flexible and Reinforced

An improved version of BUR, combining asphalt with rubber or plastic polymers for added flexibility and waterproofing. It tends to have better expansion and contraction making it suitable for temperature fluctuations. The system is resistant to punctures and tears and generally stronger than traditional BUR.

Single-Ply Membrane Roofing

Lightweight and flexible, single-ply membranes are popular due to ease of installation and energy efficiency. They come in two main types:

Thermoset (EPDM – Synthetic Rubber)

- Highly durable and cost-effective: lasts 20+ years with minimal upkeep.
- Excellent UV and weather resistance: can withstand harsh sun exposure.
- Black EPDM absorbs heat: requires reflective coatings or white options in hot climates.

Thermoplastic (TPO and PVC – Plastic-Based)

- Heat-welded seams for strength: highly resistant to leaks.
- Chemical and fire resistant: ideal for industrial environments with chemical exposure.
- TPO quality varies: some manufacturers produce inferior products, leading to performance inconsistencies.

Spray Polyurethane Foam (SPF) Roofing

SPF roofing consists of liquid polyurethane foam that is sprayed onto the roof surface, where it expands and solidifies into a continuous, durable layer. One of its greatest advantages is its high R-value, meaning it provides excellent thermal insulation, reducing heating and cooling costs in industrial buildings. The application is seamless, so it eliminates the common weak points found in membrane roofing, such as seams and fasteners, significantly lowering the risk of leaks. However, while the foam itself is highly durable, its protective coating can degrade over time, requiring periodic maintenance and reapplication to ensure long-term performance.

Metal Roofs

Metal roofs are known for their durability, longevity, and resilience in extreme weather conditions. When properly coated and maintained metal roofing systems can last 50 years or more. Their high resistance to fire, wind, and harsh environmental conditions makes them particularly attractive for industrial facilities in regions prone to severe weather. Additionally, metal roofs require minimal maintenance compared to membrane or built-up systems, making them a cost-effective solution over their lifespan. However, the higher upfront cost can be a deterrent, as metal roofing materials and installation expenses are typically greater than those of single-ply membranes or SPF systems. Furthermore, metal roofs can be prone to thermal expansion and contraction, which may lead to movement in the seams if not properly designed. Despite these trade-offs, metal flat roofs remain a top-tier choice for industrial buildings requiring long-lasting protection, minimal upkeep, and superior strength against the elements.

The different roof systems each have pros and cons, there are additional considerations that need to be considered irrespective of what type of roof a property has:

Drainage and Water Management

Flat roofs rely on internal drains, scuppers, or tapered insulation to direct water away. Poor drainage leads to ponding water, which accelerates membrane deterioration.

Roof Inspections and Preventative Maintenance

Regular roof inspections are essential for identifying early signs of damage, such as seam separation, cracks, or water intrusion, before they develop into more significant issues.

Keeping the roof clear of debris is equally important, as leaves and other obstructions can clog drains, leading to ponding water that accelerates membrane deterioration and increases the risk of leaks.

Proactively addressing minor issues as they arise helps prevent costly repairs or full roof replacements, ultimately extending the lifespan of the roofing system and minimizing operational disruptions.

Adding Solar to Industrial Roofs

The growing demand for renewable energy and operational cost savings has made solar panel installations an attractive option for industrial properties. However, integrating solar onto an industrial roof requires careful planning to avoid structural, financial, and operational pitfalls.

Here are the key considerations for solar installation:

Structural Load Capacity

Industrial buildings are not always designed to support the additional weight of solar panels, racking systems, and ballast materials.

Before installation, a structural engineering assessment is required to determine:

- If the roof can handle added weight without compromising integrity.
- Whether reinforcements are needed to prevent sagging or overloading.
- If existing HVAC systems, vents, or drainage could be obstructed.

Solar-Ready New Developments

For new industrial developments, incorporating solar-ready designs can reduce future retrofitting costs. This include:

- Reinforced roof structures: Designing for higher weight tolerance from the outset.
- Dedicated electrical infrastructure: Pre-installing conduits and inverters for seamless integration.
- Long-term roof compatibility: Selecting roofing materials that withstand solar panel mounting and penetration without premature degradation.

Fire Risks and Safety Considerations

While rare, solar panel fires have occurred due to faulty wiring, poor installation, or overheating components. Industrial owners must ensure:

- Certified installation teams: Using qualified, licensed electricians reduces wiring hazards.
- Proper panel placement: Avoiding HVAC units, vents, or highly flammable roofing materials.
- Firefighter access: Ensuring emergency personnel can safely navigate around solar arrays in the event of a fire.

Roof Repair and Solar Panel Removal Challenges

One of the most overlooked issues with solar installations is that roof repairs or replacements become significantly more complicated and expensive. Considerations include:

- Panel removal and reinstallation costs: If the roof needs repairs, solar panels must be temporarily removed and reinstalled, adding substantial labor costs.
- Warranty implications: Some roofing warranties may be voided if penetrations or additional weight compromises the membrane.
- Panel lifespan vs. roof lifespan: Solar panels typically last 25-30 years, while some industrial roofing systems may need replacement sooner, leading to misaligned timelines.

Case Study

An investor acquired a 100,000-square-foot industrial facility with a 25-year-old roof. Initially, the roof seemed serviceable, but minor leaks appeared shortly after closing. A detailed inspection revealed extensive underlying deterioration caused by years of neglected drainage maintenance. The investor faced an unexpected $350,000 roof replacement, severely impacting their projected ROI and delaying tenant occupancy by several months. The case underscores the necessity of thorough due diligence and regular preventative maintenance to avoid significant financial setbacks.

Summary

Roofs can make or break deals, making it important to do thorough inspections and confirm details of any available warranties. Insurance policies also require careful review to ensure they explicitly cover roofing-related risks, such as ponding water damage and wind uplift failures. Preventative maintenance is crucial, as neglecting early warning signs can lead to costly replacements and operational disruptions. Real-world failures consistently demonstrate that poor installation and lack of upkeep ultimately cost far more than investing in proper materials and maintenance.

22

Sprinklers

SPRINKLER SYSTEMS ARE CRITICAL for fire safety, designed to control or extinguish fires, minimize property damage, and ensure the safety of personnel. This chapter explores the different types of sprinkler systems, design considerations, and the importance of proper maintenance and testing. Here are the different types of sprinkler systems:

ESFR (Early Suppression Fast Response) Systems

Designed for high-challenge fires, such as in warehouses with high-piled storage. These systems release large volumes of water quickly to suppress fires early. ESFR systems are effective for high-pile storage without requiring in-rack sprinklers. Rapid fire suppression minimizes damage but has higher installation costs, and sufficient water supply and pressure are required.

In-Rack Sprinkler Systems

Installed directly within storage racks to provide localized fire suppression for high-rack storage areas. These systems offer additional protection in areas where overhead sprinklers may not provide adequate coverage. Note that the sprinklers can be obstructed by stored goods, requiring careful planning and maintenance.

Wet Pipe Systems

The most common type, where pipes are filled with water. When a fire triggers a sprinkler head, water is immediately discharged. Its simple design is reliable, cost-effective, and widely applicable. It's not suitable for environments where pipes might freeze.

Dry Pipe Systems

Pipes are filled with pressurized air or nitrogen. Water is released into the pipes only when the system is activated by heat from a fire, which then discharges through the open sprinklers. This system is ideal for cold storage or environments where freezing is a concern. A trade-off is a slight delay in water discharge compared to wet pipe systems.

Pre-Action Systems

Similar to dry pipe systems but require two triggers (e.g., heat and smoke detection) before water is released, reducing the risk of accidental discharge. This reduces the chance of accidental activation but comes with a higher cost and more complexity.

Deluge Systems

All sprinkler heads are open, and when activated, water discharges from all heads simultaneously. Used in high-risk areas with highly flammable materials. It provides immediate and widespread coverage but requires a reliable and high-capacity water supply.

Design Considerations

- Storage Configuration: The height and type of storage racks, distance between racks, and type of materials stored impact the sprinkler design. High-pile and rack storage often require ESFR or in-rack systems.
- Building Size and Layout: Larger buildings may require a combination of different sprinkler systems to ensure adequate coverage.
- Fire Hazard Classification: Warehouses are classified based on the fire hazard level, from low to high hazard, depending on the materials stored (e.g., combustible, flammable, or non-combustible). This classification determines the density of sprinkler heads and the required water flow rate.

Water Supply

- Water Source: Sprinkler systems must be connected to a reliable water supply, such as municipal water systems or on-site water tanks.
- Pressure and Flow Rate: Adequate water pressure and flow rate are crucial. Booster pumps may be required if the water supply lacks sufficient pressure.

Maintenance and Testing

- Regular Inspections: Sprinkler systems should be inspected regularly to ensure they are in working order. Inspections include checking for obstructions, leaks, and ensuring all components are operational.
- Testing: Systems should undergo periodic testing, including water flow tests, alarm tests, and functional tests of sprinkler heads.
- Compliance: Adhere to NFPA (National Fire Protection Association) standards, such as NFPA 13, for the design, installation, and maintenance of sprinkler systems.

Common Issues and Troubleshooting

Sprinkler systems can face several common issues such as corrosion, leaks, pipe blockage, and valve malfunctions. Regular inspections can help identify these issues early. Corrosion may occur due to moisture exposure or stagnant water in pipes, leading to leaks or blockage. Valves can malfunction due to debris or sediment accumulation. Prompt troubleshooting by trained professionals is essential to maintain system reliability and prevent costly failures.

Sprinkler System Lifespan and Replacement Costs

The lifespan of a sprinkler system varies depending on the type and maintenance quality. Wet pipe systems typically last 20–30 years with proper upkeep, while dry pipe systems may require more frequent maintenance due to corrosion from moisture and air exposure. ESFR systems and pre-action systems have similar longevity but involve higher upfront and maintenance costs. Replacement or significant maintenance costs can be substantial, often ranging from tens of thousands to several hundred thousand dollars, depending on system complexity and building size.

Impact of Building Renovations and Layout Changes

Building modifications, including changes in storage configurations or interior layouts, can significantly impact sprinkler system effectiveness and compliance. Alterations that affect storage height, rack placement, or the type of materials stored may necessitate system redesign, additional sprinkler heads, or even upgrading to a different type of sprinkler system. Such changes can be costly and must be carefully considered during planning to avoid unexpected expenditures and compliance issues.

Fire Protection Challenges

High-Rack Storage: The higher the storage racks, the more challenging it is to achieve effective sprinkler coverage. This often requires ESFR or in-rack systems.
Mixed Commodities: Warehouses storing a combination of combustible and non-combustible materials pose unique challenges for sprinkler design.
Cold Storage: Refrigerated warehouses typically require dry pipe or pre-action systems to prevent water from freezing in the pipes.

Technological Advancements

Integration with Fire Alarms and Smoke Detectors: Modern sprinkler systems can integrate with fire detection systems for enhanced response capabilities.
Smart Sprinkler Systems: These systems offer real-time monitoring and remote management, allowing for quicker detection of issues and improved maintenance.

Cost Considerations

Installation Costs: The cost of a sprinkler system varies depending on the size of the facility, the type of system, and the fire hazard classification. Initial costs can be high but are often offset by reduced insurance premiums and risk mitigation.
Retrofitting Older Buildings: Retrofitting older warehouses to meet modern fire safety standards can be costly but is essential for compliance and safety.

Case Study

A logistics company leased a large industrial facility previously used for dry storage. Unaware that their intended use—storing flammable materials—triggered stricter local fire safety regulations, they proceeded with their move. During the business license inspection, the local municipality identified the lack of an adequate sprinkler system as non-compliant with fire codes. The landlord refused to cover the expense of installing a sprinkler system, leaving the tenant solely responsible. Ultimately, the tenant had to invest a significant sum—exceeding $250,000—to install a new, compliant ESFR sprinkler system. This unexpected cost led to considerable financial strain and delays in operations, underscoring the critical importance of thoroughly understanding local regulations and ensuring clear responsibilities in lease agreements.

Summary

Sprinkler systems are vital for fire safety in industrial buildings, providing protection for both property and personnel. Selecting the appropriate system requires careful consideration of the building layout, storage configuration, and fire hazard classification. Regular maintenance, compliance with regulations, and integration with modern technologies ensure that these systems remain effective. Whether using wet pipe, ESFR, or in-rack systems, properly designed and maintained sprinkler systems are a cornerstone of warehouse safety and operational reliability.

.

23

Racking

WAREHOUSE RACKING is a fundamental component of warehouse design, enabling efficient storage, organization, and retrieval of goods. By optimizing vertical and horizontal space, racking systems play a critical role in maximizing storage capacity, improving inventory management, and enhancing operational efficiency.

Purpose of Warehouse Racking

Racking systems are designed to store materials in warehouses, helping businesses:

- Maximize Storage Capacity: Utilize both vertical and horizontal space.
- Streamline Inventory Management: Organize products for easy identification and access.
- Enhance Operational Efficiency: Reduce the time and effort required for storing and retrieving items.

Warehouse Racking Systems

Racking is a fundamental component of warehouse storage, designed to maximize space, improve accessibility, and optimize inventory management. The right system depends on factors like product type, storage density, and retrieval speed.

Some racking configurations prioritize direct access to every pallet, making them ideal for operations with a wide variety of SKUs. Others focus on high-density storage, reducing aisle space but requiring specialized equipment or specific inventory flow methods like First-In, First-Out (FIFO) or Last-In, First-Out (LIFO).

Racking systems can also accommodate different load types. Standard pallet racks work well for typical inventory, while cantilever designs support long or bulky items. Advanced setups incorporate gravity-fed movement or push-back mechanisms to enhance efficiency.

Additionally, warehouses with vertical capacity may integrate mezzanines or multi-level racking to expand storage without increasing the building footprint. The best solution depends on operational priorities, balancing accessibility, density, and overall workflow efficiency.

Design Considerations

When selecting a racking system, key factors include:

- Storage density – Balancing available space with access requirements.
- Inventory flow – Determining whether FIFO or LIFO is needed for product turnover.
- Forklift compatibility – Ensuring adequate aisle width and maneuverability.
- Load characteristics – Accounting for weight, size, and handling requirements.
- Scalability – Planning for future growth and flexibility in storage configurations.

Effective racking design aligns with warehouse operations to maximize efficiency, reduce handling time, and ensure a smooth supply chain process.

Evolution of Ceiling Heights and Racking Systems

Racking systems should maximize vertical space while adhering to the warehouse's clear ceiling height and fire safety requirements.

Warehouse design has evolved significantly over the decades, with ceiling heights playing a crucial role in shaping storage strategies. As industrial operations expanded and logistics grew more sophisticated, warehouses have continuously adapted to maximize efficiency and capacity.

1950s–1970s: Low Ceilings and Limited Racking

In the mid-20th century, warehouses were typically built with ceiling heights ranging from 12 to 16 feet. At the time, storage was largely ground-based, with minimal racking beyond basic shelving or low-rise selective pallet racks. Forklift technology was still developing, and most materials handling focused on manual labor or rudimentary lift equipment.

Racking systems were simple, often limited to single-deep selective racks, as forklifts had lower lift capacities and weren't designed to operate at significant heights. Storage density was not a primary concern since land was relatively inexpensive, and sprawling layouts were more common.

1980s–1990s: Increasing Heights and Racking Innovation

As supply chains became more complex, warehouse design shifted toward efficiency and space optimization. Ceiling heights began to rise to 20–24 feet, allowing for taller racking configurations. This period saw the broader adoption of double-deep racking and drive-in systems, enabling higher storage density within the same footprint.

The advancement of reach trucks and deep-reach forklifts allowed warehouses to stack pallets higher, leading to the increased adoption of push-back and pallet flow racking for improved inventory rotation. Logistics operations also saw more demand for bulk storage solutions, which encouraged innovations in racking to accommodate higher throughput.

2000s–2010s: High-Bay Warehouses and Automation

By the early 2000s, warehouse ceilings had climbed to 30–36 feet, driven by rising land costs and the need to maximize cubic storage. This era marked the widespread adoption of very narrow aisle (VNA) racking, which optimized aisle space and increased storage density. Specialized lift equipment, such as turret trucks, became more common, allowing operators to access racks at greater heights in tighter spaces.

E-commerce growth also played a significant role in racking evolution, leading to the expansion of mezzanine systems and multi-level picking platforms. Many warehouses began integrating automated storage and retrieval systems (AS/RS) to handle inventory at heights beyond traditional manual access.

Today: 40+ Foot Ceilings and Fully Automated Storage

Modern warehouses and distribution centers now feature ceiling heights of 40 feet or more, particularly in high-tech logistics hubs and fulfillment centers. These facilities rely heavily on automation, robotics, and AI-driven storage solutions, which have revolutionized racking design.

Figure 18: Modern Warehouse Racking

Key developments in modern racking include:

- Automated racking systems with robotic shuttles managing inventory in deep-lane storage.
- Mobile racking that eliminates static aisles by shifting entire rack structures.
- High-bay warehouses using cranes and AS/RS to handle inventory at extreme heights without human operators.

The Future: Vertical Expansion and Smart Warehousing

Looking ahead, the demand for vertical storage will continue to shape warehouse construction. Advances in robotics and artificial intelligence will allow even greater stacking heights with minimal human intervention. Multi-story warehouse designs are already emerging in dense urban areas, incorporating vertical conveyor systems, robotics, and AI-driven inventory tracking.

As racking systems continue to evolve, they will further integrate with warehouse management software (WMS), predictive analytics, and smart technology to optimize every cubic foot of space. The future of warehousing is not just taller—it's smarter.

Column Spacing and Grid Layout:

The column grid affects racking placement and forklift maneuverability. Wider spacing provides more flexibility for racking configurations.
Here are important considerations when designing a racking system:

- Load Capacity: Each racking system must handle the specific load weights of stored items. Exceeding load limits can lead to structural failure.
- Warehouse Layout: Racking should facilitate efficient workflow and easy access for forklifts or other material handling equipment.
- Aisle Width: Narrow aisles increase storage density but require specialized forklifts. Wider aisles allow for standard forklifts and easier navigation.
- Height Utilization: Optimize the full height of the warehouse while ensuring safety and accessibility. Ensure compliance with local regulations regarding maximum allowable racking height.

A significant risk with respect to racking involves safety. This is one of the biggest risks when it comes to taking over a facility with existing racking in place. Whether it's a new racking system or an existing one, here are necessary steps that need to be taken for safety and compliance:

- Certification: Requirements vary so ensure any racking is compliant with any relevant building codes and safety regulations.
- Professional Installation: Have a reputable company install the racking with quality materials.
- Engineering: A structural engineer is a helpful resource to ensure the system is safe to use as well as to confirm load capacity. This is imperative when taking over existing racking that lacks a history of certification and routine maintenance.
- Rack Inspections: Regularly inspect for damage, misaligned racks, or loose components to maintain structural integrity.
- Load Limits: Clearly mark and enforce load capacity limits to prevent collapse.
- Seismic Considerations: In earthquake-prone areas, racking

systems must meet local seismic standards to prevent tipping or collapse.

- Proper Training: Train warehouse staff on safe loading, unloading, and general racking practices to prevent accidents.
  - Repairs: Address damage promptly to ensure safety and functionality.
  - Cleaning: Keep racking areas clean and free of debris to maintain safe access.

Technological Integration

- Automation: Automated Storage and Retrieval Systems (AS/RS) use robotics to store and retrieve items, improving efficiency and reducing labor costs.
- Inventory Management: Integrate RFID tags, barcodes, or Warehouse Management Systems (WMS) for real-time inventory tracking and accuracy.

Cost Considerations

- Initial Investment: Costs vary based on the type of racking, materials used, and customization required. There may be additional costs if the building lacks sprinklers or any structural reinforcement to handle the racking. Rough estimates below.
- Long-Term Costs: Consider maintenance, repairs, and equipment needs (e.g., forklifts) when evaluating the overall cost.
- Insurance Costs: Expect an increase in insurance as the risk increases. Generally, the higher the racking goes the higher the risk, however this may be mitigated by having adhering to the steps mentioned above. As noted in the chapter on Insurance, it's advisable to have open and constant communication with your insurance advisor to address these topics in advance.
- Additional Costs: Employees will require continuous training regarding the racking and associated equipment.

Ballpark Costs for Warehouse Racking

Warehouse racking costs can vary significantly based on factors like rack type, height, depth, load capacity, material, and whether it's new or used. Below is a rough pricing guide for common racking systems:

Basic Cost Estimates (Per Pallet Position or Per Linear Foot)

Racking Type	Cost Per Pallet Position ($)	Cost Per Linear Foot ($)
Selective Racking	$50 - $80	$60 - $100
Drive-In Racking	$80 - $150	$100 - $175
Push-Back Racking	$150 - $250	$175 - $275
Pallet Flow Racking	$200 - $350	$250 - $400
Cantilever Racking	N/A	$150 - $300

Additional Cost Factors

- New vs. Used: Used racking can cost 30–50% less than new.
- Installation Costs: Typically, $2–$5 per sq. ft., but varies based on complexity.
- Permits & Engineering: Can add $1,000 – $10,000+ depending on jurisdiction.
- Seismic Compliance: In earthquake-prone areas, costs may increase 10–30% for structural reinforcements.
- Customization: Specialized coatings, colors, and materials (e.g., galvanized for cold storage) add to costs.

Real-World Estimates for Full Warehouse Setups

Racking Type	Cost / Pallet	Cost / Linear Foot	Notes
Selective Racking	$50 – $200	$60 – $150	Most common, easy access, lower cost.
Double-Deep Racking	$100 – $300	$80 – $200	Increases density but requires special forklifts.
Drive-In/Drive-Through	$150 – $500	$120 – $250	High-density storage, reduces aisle space.
Push-Back Racking	$250 – $600	$150 – $400	LIFO storage, good for high-turnover products.
Pallet Flow Racking	$300 – $1,000+	$200 – $500	FIFO system, often used for food & beverage.
Cantilever Racking	$200 – $800 per arm	N/A	Ideal for long items like lumber or pipes.
Mezzanine Racking	$15 – $40 per sq. ft.	N/A	Adds second-level storage, varies by design.
AS/RS Systems	$1,500 – $10,000+	N/A	Fully automated, varies widely based on scale.

For an accurate quote, suppliers will factor in location, size, layout, load requirements, design factors and compliance needs.

Best Practices

- Consultation: Hire a specialized racking consultant early in the process.
- Safety First: Prioritize safety in all aspects of racking design, installation, and use.
- Optimize Layout: Continuously review and adjust the racking layout to match changes in inventory or operational needs.
- Plan for Growth: Design racking systems with future expansion in mind to accommodate increased inventory.

Expert Insight

"People think because it fits together, it goes together. A properly designed and properly installed racking system has an enormous strength-to-weight ratio. I've been in warehouses where a leg in the front of a system is completely wiped out and isn't even touching the floor, yet the whole system doesn't come crashing down. If a system collapses from a minor impact, you're looking at significantly overstressed facilities or under-engineered systems. Proper engineering and installation are crucial for safety."
—Jonathan Hirst, P. Eng – Vice President and General Manager of North American Storage

Summary

Warehouse racking is an essential component of industrial real estate, enabling efficient use of space and supporting safe, organized, and effective warehouse operations. By selecting the right type of racking, optimizing layout, and ensuring proper maintenance, businesses can maximize storage capacity and operational efficiency while minimizing risks.

24

Cranes

CRANES ARE CRITICAL COMPONENTS in industrial buildings for businesses that require lifting and transporting heavy materials. They come in various designs, each suited for specific applications. This chapter explores the most common types of cranes, key considerations for their use, and best practices for ownership and maintenance.

Let's discuss the common types of cranes:

Bridge Cranes

An overhead crane that moves on a fixed rail system. The rails, often referred to as bridge ways, runways, or crane ways, allow the crane to travel long distances while handling significant weight.

Bridge cranes are designed for heavy-duty lifting which makes them ideal for large-scale manufacturing, fabrication, and heavy equipment assembly.

These are the most expensive cranes to install, particularly when factoring in that structural improvements to the building may be required to support the crane. Involve a bridge specialist early in the process to address design and installation details.

Figure 19: An Overhead Bridge Crane

Bridge Crane Capacities	
Specification	Typical Range
Capacity	1 to 500+ tons
Span (Bridge Width)	10 to 150+ feet
Lift Height	10 to 100+ feet
Common Applications	Manufacturing, steel mills, warehouses

Gantry Cranes

Similar to bridge cranes but mounted on wheels, making them mobile and versatile. Gantry cranes are designed for portability and flexibility, so they are typically smaller and lighter than bridge cranes.

Gantry cranes are used both indoors and in outdoor yards, temporary sites, or smaller indoor spaces where mobility is key. Generally, a gantry crane supports less weight compared to fixed bridge cranes, but they are significantly easier and less costly to install.

Gantry cranes are typically owned by the party that purchased and installed them, as they are mobile and not permanently attached to the building.

Gantry Crane Capacities	
Specification	Typical Range
Capacity	1 to 1,000+ tons
Span (Leg Width)	10 to 200+ feet
Lift Height	10 to 150+ feet
Common Applications	Shipping yards, rail yards, heavy manufacturing

Figure 20: A gantry crane

Jib Cranes

Fixed cranes attached to the floor, column, or wall, with a rotating arm that swings around a fixed point. Jib cranes have Limited reach and lifting capacity compared to bridge or gantry cranes, so they tend to be in workstations that require repetitive tasks or in small areas where precise lifting is needed.

Similar to Bridge cranes, jib cranes are often considered fixtures and part of the building, however the parties might agree to different terms.

Jib Crane Capacities	
Specification	Typical Range
Capacity	0.25 to 15+ tons
Boom Length (Reach)	5 to 50 feet
Lift Height	10 to 40 feet
Common Applications	Assembly lines, loading docks, maintenance areas

Figure 21: A jib crane

Key Specifications for Cranes

When assessing or installing a crane, it is essential to evaluate the following specifications:

- **Capacity:** Measured in tons or pounds, this indicates the maximum weight the crane can safely lift.
- **Below/Under Hook Height:** The distance between the floor and the center point of the hook at its highest position. This determines how high the crane can lift objects.
- **Span:** The width of the crane, measuring the distance between the rails or supports. This defines the area the crane can cover.

Figure 22: Under hook height of a crane

Ownership and Lease Considerations

Bridge cranes and jib cranes are usually considered fixtures and part of the building. Accordingly, ownership may default to the property owner unless otherwise agreed to. Gantry cranes, conversely, are moveable so ownership typically comes down to who paid for it. I would highly recommend adding a section about cranes directly to the lease, or at the very least a separate agreement between the tenant and the landlord. Include specific terms regarding crane ownership, maintenance responsibilities, and operational guidelines in the lease or a separate agreement.

The documentation should also clarify liability for damages, maintenance logs, repair costs, and certifications.

If there is no documentation, ownership of the cranes may become a civil matter and left to the courts to weigh all the evidence and decide. Not only is this process expensive and time consuming, but outcomes are also unpredictable.

Another potential challenge can arise if the tenant is leasing the crane and stops making payments on it. In most cases the leasing company will file a lien and move to repossess the crane. It may make economic sense for the landlord to negotiate with the leasing company to buy it outright, but a feasibility study would be needed. The different situations can become quite complex so I would always recommend having your attorney involved.

Maintenance, Certification and Training

- **Safety**: Always prioritize safety by adhering to maintenance schedules and addressing any issues promptly.
- **Regular Maintenance:** Cranes must be routinely inspected and maintained to ensure safe operation. This includes checking mechanical components, lubrication, and electrical systems.
- **Certification**: Regular certification by qualified specialists is mandatory to verify that the crane meets safety standards and is suitable for use. Poorly maintained or uncertified cranes may hold little value and pose significant safety risks. Before use, have a specialist inspect and certify the crane.
- **Proper Usage:** Ensure every employee who has access to the crane has been properly trained, and if required in your area, certified.

Adding a Crane to a Building

Adding a crane to a building requires careful planning and structural assessment. First, determine the crane's specifications, including its required capacity, span, and below-hook height, while ensuring the building's height can accommodate it. Additionally, evaluate whether the existing infrastructure, such as the power supply, is sufficient for crane operations. A critical step is confirming that both the building structure and the floor can support the crane's weight, dynamic loads, and operational stresses. Consulting a structural engineer and a crane specialist is essential to assess feasibility and verify load-bearing capacity. Depending on the findings, structural upgrades may be necessary, such as reinforcing beams, installing additional supports, or strengthening the foundation. It is also crucial to update the lease agreement to clarify ownership, maintenance responsibilities, and removal obligations between the landlord and tenant. In some cases, a separate agreement may be necessary to outline liability and ensure compliance with safety regulations. Lastly, the insurance provider should be notified to update the policy, ensuring proper coverage for both property damage and liability associated with crane operations.

Summary

Cranes are indispensable in many industrial applications, from heavy manufacturing to precise material handling. Whether it's a bridge crane for large-scale operations, a gantry crane for versatility, or a jib crane for focused tasks, each type serves specific needs. Understanding crane specifications, ownership implications, and maintenance requirements ensures safe and efficient operation. Always involve professionals when evaluating, installing, or certifying a crane to protect both the investment and the safety of those who rely on it.

25

Utilities

THIS CHAPTER EXPLORES the common utilities in industrial real estate, alternative solutions for properties lacking municipal services, and key considerations to effectively manage utilities.

Common Utilities in Industrial Properties

Industrial properties rely heavily on various utilities to ensure seamless and efficient operations. Understanding these utilities enables owners and tenants to plan strategically and meet both current and future operational requirements.

Electricity

Electricity powers machinery, lighting, HVAC systems, and critical equipment. Many industrial facilities require robust three-phase power infrastructure to accommodate high-energy machinery and processes. Electrical capacity, measured in kilovolt-amperes (kVA), must align closely with operational demands to avoid disruptions or costly upgrades. Backup generators, whether diesel, natural gas, or battery-based, provide crucial redundancy in operations where power interruptions are unacceptable. (Refer to Chapter 18 for more details on electricity.)

Water Supply

Water is vital for industrial processes, sanitation, and fire suppression systems. Industrial facilities typically require high-capacity water lines with consistent pressure. Depending on the industry, additional water treatment or filtration may be necessary to comply with regulatory standards or operational specifications. Facilities with inadequate municipal water supply may need to consider alternative solutions like private wells, rainwater harvesting, or bulk water delivery.

Natural Gas

Natural gas commonly fuels heating systems, manufacturing processes, and specialized equipment. Ensuring sufficient gas line availability and capacity is critical, particularly for industries with high thermal demands, such as foundries, food processing plants, and chemical manufacturing facilities. Evaluating gas infrastructure during property assessments helps mitigate future operational risks.

Sewer and Wastewater Management

Industrial operations often produce significant volumes of wastewater, requiring careful management to maintain regulatory compliance and environmental protection. Facilities disconnected from municipal sewers may need on-site wastewater solutions, including septic systems, wastewater treatment plants, or holding tanks. Permits for wastewater discharge are frequently necessary, and compliance monitoring is typically stringent.

Telecommunications and Internet

Reliable high-speed internet connectivity is indispensable for automation, IoT systems, real-time inventory management, and remote monitoring. Fiber-optic connections are typically preferred for their reliability, bandwidth capacity, and low latency. In areas lacking sufficient infrastructure, alternative solutions such as satellite or fixed wireless internet may be considered, though these may involve trade-offs in speed or reliability.

Compressed Air Systems

Compressed air is essential in many industrial processes for operating pneumatic tools, machinery, and process control systems. Facilities with built-in infrastructure for air lines and compressors benefit from reduced installation costs and operational efficiencies.

Specialized Utilities

Certain industrial properties may require specialized utilities, including steam and chilled water systems for manufacturing processes, bulk storage facilities for fuels, chemicals, or industrial gases, and advanced infrastructure for regulatory compliance and safety.

Key Considerations for Utilities

Capacity and Scalability

Utility infrastructure must align with current operational requirements while allowing for future growth. Evaluating existing power supply, water systems, gas capacity, and telecommunications infrastructure during due diligence prevents costly surprises.

Redundancy and Reliability

Utility disruptions can cause significant operational downtime and financial losses. Implementing robust backup systems, such as emergency generators, secondary water storage tanks, and redundant communication lines, enhances resilience and reliability.

Backup Power and Emergency Preparedness

Backup power systems like diesel, natural gas, or battery-based generators are essential for facilities that cannot afford operational interruptions. Diesel generators provide reliability and rapid startup capabilities, while natural gas generators offer cleaner emissions and ease of fuel access. Regular maintenance, testing, and an emergency preparedness plan are critical for operational continuity.

Regulatory Compliance

All utilities must comply with local, state/provincial, and federal regulations. Particular attention should be paid to wastewater treatment permits, environmental discharge standards, and utility easements or rights-of-way.

Cost Implications

Utilities represent a substantial operating expense. Understanding rate structures, peak demand charges, and leveraging cost-saving strategies such as energy-efficient systems, renewable energy installations, or water conservation technologies can significantly impact the bottom line.

Infrastructure Condition and Maintenance

Aging utility systems can incur high maintenance costs and operational inefficiencies. Regular assessments and proactive maintenance planning can extend utility lifespan, minimize emergency repairs, and reduce operational downtime.

Utility Easements and Rights-of-Way

Utility easements permit service providers to access property for installing, maintaining, or upgrading utilities. These easements can restrict property usage, affect expansion plans, and influence property valuation. Thoroughly reviewing title documents and negotiating easements proactively mitigates future operational challenges.

Tenant-Specific Requirements

Different industries present unique utility needs, from high electrical demands to specialized gas line installations. Industrial properties should remain flexible, accommodating necessary utility upgrades to attract and retain tenants.

Accessibility for Upgrades

Utility infrastructure should be designed for easy access to facilitate maintenance and future upgrades. Poorly positioned or buried utilities can significantly complicate and increase the cost of necessary improvements.

Case Study: Utility Enhancements in a Distribution Center

An e-commerce tenant required substantial electrical capacity for automated sorting equipment and reliable fiber-optic internet for inventory management systems. Recognizing these needs, the landlord upgraded the facility's electrical capacity from 600 kVA to 1200 kVA and coordinated fiber-optic internet installation with a local provider. These proactive enhancements ensured operational efficiency, tenant satisfaction, and increased property value.

Alternative Solutions for Non-Municipal Services

When municipal water and sewer connections are unavailable, industrial property owners must adopt alternative solutions such as private wells, rainwater harvesting, bulk water delivery, septic systems, wastewater treatment plants, or holding tanks. These solutions, commonly used in agricultural and rural contexts, have well-established infrastructure and support networks, providing viable operational continuity.

Water Supply Alternatives

Private Wells

Private wells provide on-site groundwater access, reducing reliance on municipal water sources. However, they require permits, testing, and treatment to ensure water quality and regulatory compliance.

Cost Considerations:

- Drilling & Installation: $10,000 - $100,000+ (varies by depth and geology)
- Filtration & Treatment: $5,000 - $50,000 (depending on water quality needs)
- Annual Maintenance & Testing: $500 - $5,000

Regulatory Challenges:

- Water Rights & Permits: In some states (e.g., California & Texas), groundwater usage is regulated, and permits may limit withdrawal amounts.
- Contamination Risk: Wells near industrial sites require regular testing for heavy metals, nitrates, and bacterial contamination (EPA and local health department oversight).
- Well Abandonment Rules: If a well is decommissioned, it must be sealed properly to prevent groundwater contamination (regulated by state water agencies).

Example: A food processing plant in rural Texas relies on a private well for production. However, due to high iron content, they installed reverse osmosis filtration, adding $50,000 in treatment costs.

Example: A concrete batch plant in Arizona uses groundwater for mixing concrete. High salinity required a softening system, increasing their operating costs by 15% annually.

Rainwater Harvesting

Rainwater collection systems supplement water supply for non-potable uses, reducing municipal demand. However, large-scale industrial systems face infrastructure costs and regulatory hurdles.

Cost Considerations:

- Installation (Tanks, Gutters, & Filtration): $20,000 - $500,000+
- Storage Tanks (Cisterns): $0.50 - $5 per gallon of capacity
- Filtration & UV Treatment: $2,000 - $50,000

Regulatory Challenges:

- State & Local Restrictions: Some areas, like Colorado (historically), Nevada, and Utah, have restrictions on capturing rainwater, as it affects downstream users' water rights.
- Water Quality Standards: If used for industrial cooling or sanitation, rainwater must meet local health codes and EPA guidelines.
- Backflow Prevention: Many municipalities require backflow prevention devices to ensure harvested water doesn't contaminate potable supplies.

Example 1: A large distribution warehouse in Florida collects rainwater for truck washing & irrigation, saving $100,000 annually in municipal water fees.

Example 2: An auto manufacturing plant in Germany integrates rainwater harvesting into cooling systems. Due to local laws, they had to install extensive filtration, increasing upfront costs by 25%.

Bulk Water Delivery

For remote facilities without groundwater or municipal access, water must be trucked in and stored on-site. This is the most expensive option but is sometimes the only viable solution.

Cost Considerations:

- Water Delivery: $0.01 - $0.10 per gallon (varies by region & distance)
- Storage Tanks (Cisterns): $1,000 - $100,000 (above or below ground)
- Pump Systems: $5,000 - $50,000

Cost Comparison:

- A facility using 10,000 gallons per day could spend $100 - $1,000 per day on delivered water.
- Over a year, costs range from $36,500 - $365,000+, making this far more expensive than well or rainwater options.

Regulatory Challenges:

- Water Quality Testing: Bulk water must comply with FDA, EPA, and local health standards, especially for food-related or medical industries.
- Storage Regulations: Some states (e.g., California & Arizona) require secondary containment to prevent leaks into groundwater.
- Emergency Supply Limitations: Delivery can be disrupted by weather, fuel shortages, or road conditions, leading to operational risks.

Example: A remote mining site in Nevada spends $250,000 annually on trucked-in water. To reduce costs, they installed a small-scale desalination unit to purify brackish groundwater.

Example: A data center in the Middle East relies on bulk water delivery for cooling systems. To manage costs, they optimized water reuse and installed on-site filtration, cutting delivery expenses by 30%.

Sewer and Wastewater Management

Proper wastewater management is critical for industrial facilities to ensure regulatory compliance, environmental protection, and operational efficiency. The appropriate method depends on wastewater volume, treatment needs, land availability, and cost considerations.

Septic Systems

Septic systems are on-site wastewater treatment solutions typically used in areas without municipal sewer connections. They rely on a combination of septic tanks and drain fields to process and filter wastewater naturally. Here are a few key considerations:

- Land Requirements: Drain fields require adequate space for wastewater absorption.
- Maintenance Needs: Tanks must be pumped every 3–5 years to remove solids and prevent system failure.
- Capacity Limitations: Best suited for low-to-moderate wastewater volumes; industrial users with high discharge may overwhelm the system.
- Soil Suitability: Percolation tests determine if the soil can effectively absorb treated water.

Example: A small manufacturing facility in rural Alberta installs a 1,500-gallon septic system due to the lack of municipal sewer access.

Example: A truck repair shop in a suburban area uses a septic system but adds a grease interceptor to prevent oil contamination in the drain field.

Cost Estimate: $5,000 - $50,000+ (varies by size and soil conditions)

Regulatory Challenge: Septic systems must meet local health department standards and may require regular inspections to prevent groundwater contamination.

On-Site Wastewater Treatment Plants (WWTPs)

Larger industrial facilities with significant wastewater volumes often build on-site wastewater treatment plants (WWTPs) to process and discharge wastewater safely. These systems can treat chemical, biological, and heavy metal contaminants before disposal or reuse. Key considerations here:

- Customization: Designed to treat specific wastewater contaminants based on industrial processes.
- High Initial Investment: Costly to install but reduces long-term disposal fees.
- Permit & Compliance: Requires EPA & state environmental permits for operation and discharge.
- Wastewater Recycling: Treated water can be reused for cooling, irrigation, or processing.

Example: A brewery in California installs an on-site WWTP to process wastewater and recycles it for equipment cleaning and irrigation.

Example: A pharmaceutical plant uses a membrane bioreactor (MBR) in its on-site WWTP to filter out bacteria and pharmaceuticals before releasing water into the municipal system.

Cost Estimate: $500,000 - $10 million+ (depending on complexity and scale)

Regulatory Challenge: Strict monitoring and reporting are required to comply with federal and state wastewater discharge regulations.

Holding Tanks

Holding tanks store wastewater temporarily before it is pumped out and transported to an off-site treatment facility. These tanks are sealed to prevent leakage and are ideal for low-volume, intermittent wastewater generation. Here are things to consider:

- Temporary Solution: Used when sewer connections or treatment systems are unavailable.
- High Ongoing Costs: Requires frequent pumping and disposal (cost per gallon).
- Regulatory Compliance: Stored wastewater must be properly contained and documented for legal disposal.

Example: A construction site in New York installs a 10,000-gallon holding tank for restroom and wash station wastewater until permanent sewer connections are available.

Example: A pop-up food processing facility uses a holding tank for wastewater storage and schedules weekly pumping services.

Cost Estimate: $1,500 - $10,000 (tank installation) + $0.05 - $0.50 per gallon for pumping services

Regulatory Challenge: Disposal records and proper transport permits are required to prevent illegal dumping.

Summary

Utilities are the backbone of any industrial property, influencing its functionality, tenant appeal, and value. By assessing utility infrastructure, capacity, and compliance, stakeholders can ensure that the property meets current and future demands while minimizing risks and costs. For properties lacking municipal services, alternative solutions like private wells or septic systems can ensure continued operation. A proactive approach to utilities enhances property performance and supports long-term success in industrial real estate.

26

Drainage

EFFECTIVE DRAINAGE SYSTEMS, both at the building and property levels, are essential for the functionality, safety, and longevity of industrial properties. Proper management of water—whether stormwater, wastewater, or process water—is crucial for operational efficiency and regulatory compliance. This chapter explores the components of drainage systems, and the considerations required for effective design, installation, and maintenance.

Building-Level Drainage Systems

Floor Drains

Collects water from spills, cleaning, or equipment operation and directs it to the drainage network. Flor drains are common in manufacturing areas, warehouses, and loading docks. Drains will typically have grates or covers to prevent debris from entering the system.

Trench Drains

Linear drains designed to handle large volumes of water over expansive areas. These are ideal for loading bays, processing areas, or high-traffic zones prone to water accumulation.

Figure 23: Trench drain

Sump Systems

- Dry Sumps: Collect water for removal by manual or pump methods.
- Wet Sumps: Hold water before being pumped to treatment or disposal systems.
- Dual Compartment Sumps: Feature sections for sediment separation or oil-water separation.

Oil-Water Separators: Remove hydrocarbons and oils from wastewater before discharge into municipal systems. These are required for properties handling machinery, vehicles, or industrial fluids. Note these must comply with local environmental discharge standards.

Roof Drainage Systems

A well-designed roof drainage system is essential for preventing water pooling, leaks, and structural damage by efficiently diverting rainwater away from the building. These systems typically consist of roof drains, scuppers, gutters, and downspouts, all working together to manage water flow effectively.

For flat or low-slope roofs, minor slopes are often incorporated to guide water toward drains and prevent standing water, which can lead to long-term structural issues.

Key Considerations

- Capacity & Flow Management: the system must be designed to handle peak water volumes, including unexpected spills or cleaning runoff.
- Material Durability: industrial environments require corrosion-resistant materials that can withstand exposure to chemicals, extreme temperatures, and heavy rainfall.
- Accessibility for Maintenance: proper drainage design should include cleanouts and access points to allow for routine inspections and debris removal.
- Regulatory Compliance: drainage systems must meet building codes and wastewater management regulations, ensuring that runoff is properly managed without causing environmental concerns.
- Integration with Property Drainage: the system should connect seamlessly with on-site stormwater management to prevent backups or overflows that could affect the facility's operations.

By prioritizing capacity, durability, compliance, and integration, an effective roof drainage system helps protect the building's structure, prevent costly repairs, and maintain operational efficiency in industrial facilities.

Property-Level Drainage Systems

Effective property-level drainage is crucial for managing stormwater, preventing flooding, and ensuring compliance with environmental regulations. Proper site design helps direct water away from critical areas, reducing the risk of erosion, foundation damage, and operational disruptions.

Stormwater Management Strategies

- Surface Water Flow: the site should be graded and sloped to naturally direct water away from the property. Features such as swales, curbs, and berms help control and guide runoff efficiently.
- Retention Ponds: hold water permanently, gradually releasing it into the environment to prevent excessive discharge.
- Detention Ponds: temporarily store stormwater, slowing its flow rate before it enters drainage systems.
- Irrigation Systems: reusing stormwater for landscaping or non-potable applications can reduce water consumption. Filtration systems should be incorporated to maintain water quality before reuse.
- Drainage Infrastructure: installing catch basins, culverts, and storm drains prevents water pooling and minimizes flood risks during heavy rain.

Key Considerations

- Grading & Slope Design: the landscape should be engineered to naturally direct stormwater away from buildings and high-traffic areas.
- Permeable Surfaces: using permeable paving materials can reduce runoff and improve groundwater recharge.
- Environmental Compliance: drainage systems must meet stormwater discharge and pollution control regulations to prevent contamination of nearby water sources.
- Routine Maintenance: regularly clearing debris from storm drains, retention ponds, and culverts helps maintain system efficiency and prevents blockages.

A well-planned property-level drainage system ensures stormwater is managed effectively, protects the site from flooding, and supports sustainable water use within industrial and commercial properties.

Challenges and Mitigation Strategies

Clogs and Blockages

- Cause: Accumulation of debris, grease, or sediment.
- Solution: Implement regular inspections and cleaning schedules.

Flooding and Backflow

- Cause: Overloaded systems during heavy rainfall or improper design.
- Solution: Install backflow preventers and overflow mechanisms.

Aging Infrastructure

- Cause: Older systems may not meet current demands.
- Solution: Retrofit or upgrade systems during property improvements.

Environmental Regulations

- Challenge: Compliance with stricter discharge standards.
- Solution: Install pre-treatment systems, such as oil-water separators or sediment filters.

Case Study: Stormwater Management for an Industrial Park

A 200,000-square-foot industrial park faced challenges with pooling water during heavy rains. The property owner installed a stormwater management system, including retention ponds and a network of trench drains, to redirect water efficiently. Grading improvements and permeable paving reduced runoff, while the addition of oil-water separators ensured compliance with local environmental regulations. These upgrades minimized flooding risks, reduced liability, and enhanced tenant satisfaction.

Summary

Drainage systems at both the building and property levels are fundamental to the functionality and safety of industrial properties. Properly designed and maintained systems ensure effective water management, regulatory compliance, and protection against flooding or contamination. By addressing both internal and external drainage needs, owners can safeguard their investments and provide reliable infrastructure for tenants.

However, it's equally important that tenants understand their role in managing drainage as well. Even the most well-engineered system can fail if it's misused or neglected. Tenants should avoid blocking drains, improperly disposing of materials, or allowing debris to accumulate in outdoor areas. Water is one of the most quietly destructive forces in industrial real estate—it can erode concrete, damage foundations, compromise structural integrity, and lead to mold or hazardous working conditions. A single overlooked drainage issue can result in significant downtime and costly repairs. Shared responsibility between landlords and tenants is crucial to keeping systems functioning as intended.

27

Insurance

INDUSTRIAL PROPERTIES FACE A UNIQUE set of risks, making proper insurance coverage essential for property owners, tenants, and investors. This chapter explores the key types of insurance, risk factors, policy considerations, and how insurance integrates with lease agreements to ensure comprehensive protection.

This chapter was written by Skylar Romines, the founder of ATW Advisors. With a wealth of experience in the insurance industry and a passion for advocating on behalf of business owners, Skylar founded ATW Advisors to fill a critical gap in the market. Skylar can be found on X at @skylarromines or at www.atwadvisors.com.

Insurance for commercial real estate owners and investors is uniquely impacted by factors like replacement cost valuations, catastrophic weather events, inflation and economic volatility, reinsurance challenges and evolving risks, such as cyber.

Industrial real estate is a cornerstone of modern commerce. As these properties are vital to supply chains and production processes, protecting them against unforeseen risks is paramount. Insurance for industrial real estate provides financial security by mitigating potential losses from potential losses like property damage, liability claims, and business interruption. This chapter explores the key types of insurance coverage, factors influencing premiums, and strategies for effective risk management.

Industrial Real Estate is Not One Thing

Other classes of real estate look homogenous. An apartment is an apartment. Retail is retail. A hotel is a hotel. Industrial real estate is everything from data centers to trampoline parks.

Here are some of the most common types of industrial real estate and concerns underwriters may have about each type:

Warehouses and Distribution Centers

General Warehouses: Primarily used for storage, with limited movement of goods. They often have lower door-to-square-footage ratios and may include cold storage for perishable items.
Distribution Warehouses: Focused on shipping goods efficiently from a central location, typically large, one-story buildings (50,000+ square feet).
Bulk Warehouses: The largest type, ranging from 50,000 to over 1 million square feet, designed for regional distribution and often located outside metro areas.
Risk of Inventory Damage: Underwriters assess the value and type of goods stored, exposure to theft, fire, or water damage, and the adequacy of security measures.
Building Construction: Factors like roof integrity, fire suppression systems, and structural resilience against natural disasters (e.g., floods or earthquakes) are critical.
Warehouse Legal Liability: Coverage for goods damaged due to negligence during storage or handling is essential.

Manufacturing Facilities

Heavy Manufacturing: Large, capital-intensive facilities with specialized equipment for industries like steel production or shipbuilding. These properties require significant power supply and infrastructure.
Light Manufacturing: Smaller facilities focused on assembling or producing smaller parts using portable equipment. These are more flexible and easier to reconfigure for new tenants.
Equipment Breakdown: Machinery and equipment are high-value assets; underwriters focus on coverage for mechanical failures or electrical issues.
Hazardous Operations: Heavy manufacturing may involve flammable materials or high-risk processes like welding. These require specialized risk assessments.
Environmental Risks: Facilities located in flood-prone or high-risk areas face higher premiums due to potential damage from natural disasters.
Product Liability: Risks associated with defective products or recalls are significant for manufacturers and influence policy terms.

Cold Storage/ Refrigeration Facilities

Designed for temperature-sensitive goods such as food or pharmaceuticals. These facilities include refrigeration systems and accommodate large trucks and machinery for distribution.

Temperature Control Systems: Underwriters evaluate refrigeration reliability, backup systems, and risks of spoilage due to power outages.
Perishable Inventory: High-value goods like pharmaceuticals or food require coverage for losses due to temperature fluctuations or contamination.
Utility Failures: Business interruption insurance is vital to mitigate losses from extended downtime caused by utility disruptions.

Flex Space

Multi-purpose buildings combining office, warehousing, light manufacturing, or showroom space. They feature lower ceilings (typically under 18 feet) and are highly adaptable to tenant needs.

Multi-Tenant Risks: Shared spaces may have overlapping liabilities among tenants; underwriters analyze lease agreements and liability allocations.
Adaptability of Use: Frequent changes in use (e.g., office vs. light manufacturing) can introduce varying risks that need careful evaluation.
Fire Protection Systems: Adequate fire suppression is crucial, especially if tenants engage in activities involving flammable materials.

Showroom Buildings

A hybrid of retail and industrial space, where products are displayed and stored on-site. Common examples include car dealerships, with at least 50% of the space dedicated to showcasing products.

Customer Safety: Liability risks related to customer injuries on premises are a key consideration for underwriters.
Inventory Display Risks: Theft or damage to displayed goods requires comprehensive property insurance coverage.
Hybrid Use Exposures: Combining retail with storage may introduce unique risks requiring tailored policies.

Research and Development (R&D) Facilities

Tailored for technology-driven industries, these properties combine office, manufacturing, and warehouse spaces. They are often located in campus-like settings with ample parking.

Specialized Equipment Coverage: High-value lab equipment requires insurance against breakdowns or accidental damage.

Intellectual Property Risks: Coverage for patent disputes or financial losses due to stolen designs is increasingly relevant for tech-driven industries.

Facility Location: Proximity to high-risk zones (e.g., flood-prone areas) impacts premiums significantly.

Data Centers

Highly specialized facilities housing servers and telecom equipment. They require significant power capacity and reinforced structures to support heavy equipment loads.

The condition of the buildings can also heavily impact underwriting decisions. Class A modern buildings with premium features may be more agreeable than class B buildings that are older, even if well maintained. Class C buildings that are aging and often have deferred maintenance issues are often more difficult to insure. Issues like vacancy can also impact an asset's insurability.

Cyber Liability Insurance: Protects against data breaches, ransomware attacks, and IT system failures that can disrupt operations.

Power Supply Reliability: Underwriters assess backup generators and energy redundancy systems critical for uninterrupted operations.

Structural Integrity: Reinforced buildings capable of handling heavy equipment loads are essential considerations for underwriting property insurance.

Outside of the type of industrial real estate, there are also general considerations that will impact insurance premiums:

Factors Influencing Insurance Premiums

The cost of insuring industrial properties depends on several variables:

Location: Proximity to natural hazards (e.g., flood zones or earthquake-prone areas) or high-crime regions significantly impacts premiums.

Building Characteristics: The age, construction type (e.g., fire-resistant materials), and condition of the property are critical factors. Older buildings or those with outdated safety features typically incur higher premiums.

Tenant Operations: The nature of tenants' businesses plays a significant role. High-risk activities such as chemical storage or heavy manufacturing elevate premiums due to increased accident potential.

Safety Features: Properties equipped with advanced safety systems—like fire suppression systems, security alarms, and proper ventilation—may qualify for lower rates.

Claims History: A history of frequent claims can lead to higher premiums as insurers perceive greater risk.

Types of Insurance Coverage for Industrial Real Estate

A robust insurance plan for industrial properties typically includes multiple coverage types tailored to address unique risks associated with these assets.

This likely includes Property insurance, which is a foundational coverage protects the physical structure of the building, including walls, roofs, and permanently installed machinery. It ensures financial recovery in case of damage caused by fire, theft, vandalism, or natural disasters like storms. Property insurance can be covered by the tenant or the landlord.

Liability insurance safeguards property owners against claims related to bodily injury or property damage occurring on the premises. Given the presence of heavy machinery and high-risk activities in industrial settings, this coverage is essential to mitigate legal and financial repercussions.

There are also peripheral coverages that may be considered, depending on location and specific risks:

Flood Insurance: Protects against water damage in flood-prone areas.

Earthquake Insurance: Covers damages from seismic activities.

Environmental Liability Insurance: Addresses risks associated with hazardous materials or contamination.

Cyber, Data Breach and Privacy Liability: Provide defense & indemnity for failure to safeguard confidential data, and damage to owned equipment from outside attacks.

Directors and officers: Protects the people who serve as directors or officers from personal losses if they are sued by the organization's employees, customers, vendors or other parties.

There are factors within an owner operator's control that can help with both cost containment and procurement of appropriate coverage. Some of these considerations are:

Key Risks and Risk Management Strategies

Industrial properties face a range of risks that require proactive management to minimize insurance claims and ensure long-term asset protection.

Fire Hazards

- Fire remains one of the most significant threats to industrial facilities due to machinery operation and storage of flammable materials.
- Regularly inspect electrical systems.
- Install fire suppression systems.
- Conduct fire drills and training for tenants.

Environmental Risks

- Industrial operations often involve hazardous substances that may lead to environmental contamination.
- Ensure compliance with environmental regulations.
- Provide proper storage facilities for chemicals.
- Develop spill response protocols.

Natural Disasters

- Floods, earthquakes, and storms can cause extensive damage.
- Assess geographical risks before purchasing insurance.
- Retrofit buildings to withstand earthquakes if located in seismic zones.
- Maintain drainage systems to prevent flooding.

Tenant Safety Protocols

- Tenants' adherence to safety standards is crucial for reducing liability risks.

- Mandate personal protective equipment (PPE) use.
- Conduct regular safety audits.
- Include safety requirements in lease agreements.

Navigating the Insurance Market

Selecting the right insurance policy requires careful evaluation of coverage options and collaboration with experienced brokers who understand industrial real estate's unique needs. As the market continues to evolve, having a third-party consultant such as an owner's rep working with the broker also creates a unique advantage for insurance procurement.

Working with Specialized Brokers

Specialized brokers can help identify appropriate policies based on property type, location, and tenant operations. They also assist in negotiating competitive premiums by leveraging their relationships with insurers.

Customizing Policies

A one-size-fits-all approach does not work for industrial properties. Tailored policies ensure comprehensive protection without overpaying for unnecessary coverage.

Reviewing Policies Annually

As tenant operations or property conditions change over time, annual policy reviews ensure continued adequacy of coverage.

Future Trends in Industrial Real Estate Insurance

As industrial real estate evolves with advancements like automation and green building technologies, insurance policies are adapting:

Cybersecurity Coverage: With increased reliance on automated systems and IoT devices, cybersecurity insurance is becoming integral to protect against data breaches or system failures caused by cyberattacks.

Adverse Weather Events Adaptation: Insurers are factoring severe weather events into risk assessments more aggressively, leading to new policy structures tailored for extreme weather events.

Liability Insurance Evolving

As insurers continue to tighten underwriting guidelines surrounding liability insurance, there is a bifurcation of rating in industrial real estate. Assets with high exposure to the public and potential litigated claims from incidents like trips and falls (e.g. trampoline parks) are likely to continue to carry higher rates, whereas other types of industrial real estate (e.g. warehouses) are likely to be less impacted.

28

Legal Considerations

LET'S TALK ABOUT the law. This chapter is going to cover the typical legal documents that you encounter in industrial real estate.

This chapter was written by Ron Rohde, a commercial real estate attorney for the past 15 years who specializes in Purchase and Sale Agreements and NNN leasing. Ron also owns and directly operate 8 NNN industrial properties of over 150,000 square feet and 14 acres of IOS in DFW, Texas.

Lease Agreements

The lease is the agreement between a landlord and the tenant. It is a critical piece of the industrial real estate investment because it governs the stream of income payments that you expect to receive. Beyond basic terms such as rent, term, renewals, reimbursements, industrial real estate leases are highly sensitive to permitted use and operations on the property. Whether its environmental concerns, city compliance, or just following the rules in a multi-tenant property, the lease is critical to understand what the tenant can and cannot do.

NNN Lease: The standard lease agreement will be a "triple net" (NNN) lease which can be applied to all industrial asset types. They are market standard for any property beyond the earliest investor. The second most common lease will be a gross lease. This permits the tenant to pay a single amount each month and requires the landlord to shoulder the burden of risk of increase in property taxes, insurance premiums and operating expenses.
Gross Leases: These are more common in flex properties with less sophisticated tenants. Gross leases hold the landlord responsible for property taxes, insurance, and maintenance costs. They typically have shorter terms and no renewal options to protect the landlord. This forces the parties back

to negotiate what a market rent should be every few years. One of the best ways to add value is by purchasing a gross leased property and converting the tenants into NNN leases.

Tenant Responsibilities vs. Landlord Obligations: This part of the lease deals with specifying both physical repair obligations as well as financial obligations. For every type of repair, there will be a party responsible for inspecting, getting bids, approving a contractor and ensuring the repair is completed. This is separate from the party responsible for paying for said repair. When reviewing leases, be sure to understand how this clause impacts your financial modeling and your time or management projections.

Default & Remedies: What happens if a Tenant misses a rent payment? Violate a parking rule? Default often comes in multiple levels, with different cure periods and landlord remedies based on the type of default. Your lawyer will likely advise on how to file for a judicial eviction but be aware of lengthy universal cure periods (even for late rent). I advise my clients to always understand the cost and time for an eviction based on the asset type and lease terms. As an investor, knowledge is power and knowing how quickly or costly an eviction may be is critical information when negotiating with a defaulting tenant.

Real estate investors must know your leases, industrial leases tend to fit within form versions, but nothing can ever be relied upon as "standard." For example, one of the biggest issues comes with outdoor storage. Usual leases charge a rate per square foot of the building. While the broker may quote a price per acre and a total monthly base rent, the lease itself may calculate an extremely high per square foot rate to accommodate the yard usage. Disputes arise

Insurance

Understanding your insurance coverage (what is covered and what is not as well as establishing your own legal procedures and policies internally are the most important aspects of being an industrial property owner. The two main types of insurance coverage are property coverage (insuring the improvements) and liability coverage (insuring the owner). The amount of property coverage is typically determined by your lender, they will specify the amounts and types of coverage and there must be prompt communication between the loan document requirements and your insurance broker. More sophisticated investors will understand how to adjust coverage to save money while complying with loan documents.

Liability insurance protects the investor from third parties, these are primarily invitees (people invited onto the property) and trespassers (people who were not invited). Its arguable more important to protect against liability risk because its a more difficult to control type of risk. We can understand the replacement cost of a building or improvement and take steps to mitigate it, but third parties can cause or injure themselves in a manner that is unforeseeable. Ultimately, understanding what factors contribute to both premiums and legal procedures to mitigate or handle insurance events is crucial to developing a solid industrial accident program. Liability Protection for Landlords & Tenants (Managing legal exposure) Property Insurance & Business Interruption Coverage (Legal considerations for industrial property insurance)

Will the Tenant cover premiums for BI? Your lease will need to specify whether a tenant reimbursement for business interruption coverage is included or not. Most basic leases will only require the tenant to reimburse premium costs for casualty and general liability policies, but savvy investors can include any type of policy.

Tenant-Specific Legal Concerns

Industrial tenants require a different approach as compared to residential, retail or office. It creates a deeper understanding of the creative problem solving that landlords and tenants face. Industrial tenants tend to be less demanding of their landlords relative to other asset classes. While the lease requirements may contain identical language requiring a roof to be "watertight," I've found that a retail tenant will be utilizing 100% of their space and placing sensitive inventory directly in the line of fire. Whereas an industrial tenant may be storing packaged goods, metal components or other items that inherently have a layer of protection prior to incurring damage from a leaking roof.

Industrial tenants also tend to require and install very expensive equipment and modifications to the property. This extensive investment creates one of the best features of industrial investment: sticky tenants.

While we may already appreciate the moving costs and difficulties in relocating equipment, the language in your lease can also allow the landlord to keep any expensive equipment that the tenant has paid for and installed. Its common for the landlord to retain such equipment when a tenant vacates and it helps attract a new tenant with that equipment; think gantry cranes, custom racks or worktables.

In addition, you'll want to understand how your tenant intends to use the space. This is where the unique aspect of industrial can be more of a challenge compared to other asset classes. Industrial tenants may not fit neatly into a "warehousing" or "distribution" bucket, instead they may combine elements of light assembly with partial warehousing and internal distribution uses.

Be sure that your lease contemplates the expected use, but also that you control what the tenant does on your property. It can be a fine line, but goal seeking to produce clarity on the permitted use (assembly, but no chemical cleaning, manufacturing, but not motors exceeding 100hp for noise) will ensure a cooperative relationship.

Exit Strategies & Disposition Legal Risks

Once you've created value, investors in industrial will look to sell. The biggest mistakes I see industrial investors make is not preparing enough for the due diligence requests that occur after signing the sale agreement. For example, tenant estoppels will likely be required for all tenants to confirm the lease terms, rental rate and no outstanding claims against the landlord. But few of my clients check with tenants that the tenant assumptions match the landlords. Instead, we wait until receiving a signed estoppel back from the tenant and deal with the discrepancy then.

In addition, site visits and looking for potential environmental concerns before showing the property to prospective buyers can greatly improve the odds of a smooth environmental inspection. If you go walk the property and remove any discarded tires, that is an easy way to avoid a common REC.

Additional Considerations:

Permitting & Regulatory Approvals

This process is often fraught with legal interpretation, thick applications and strict definitions of permitted uses. Its critical to stay informed about permitting and zoning changes as they can drastically impact the value of your industrial property.

Change of Use Implications (considerations for converting properties to non-industrial uses)

This is one niche of industrial investing that can yield astronomical returns.

If you can obtain zoning changes or denser use permissions, you can create millions of dollars of value to existing parcels.

Environmental Regulations & Restrictions

Understand and ensure compliance with local, state, and federal regulations related to pollution control, hazardous materials storage, emissions standards, and environmental impact assessments. Conduct regular audits and maintain detailed records to demonstrate ongoing adherence to environmental laws.

Brownfield Redevelopment & Contaminated Sites

Assess and manage potential legal liabilities and compliance requirements associated with previously contaminated properties. Engage environmental specialists to perform thorough site assessments (Phase I and Phase II ESAs), remediation planning, and monitoring to mitigate environmental risks and liabilities. Leverage available incentives and grants aimed at revitalizing brownfield sites to enhance project feasibility and profitability.

OSHA Regulations

Ensure strict adherence to Occupational Safety and Health Administration (OSHA) standards, covering a wide range of safety protocols necessary for maintaining safe warehouse and industrial environments. Regularly train staff on safety procedures, emergency response actions, and hazard recognition. Maintain clear documentation of training records, inspections, and incident reports. Conduct periodic facility safety audits to proactively identify and correct potential hazards. Develop comprehensive workplace safety programs, including ergonomic considerations, proper equipment handling, personal protective equipment (PPE) usage, and effective communication of safety guidelines to all personnel.

ADA Compliance

When applying for a new certificate of occupancy, bringing an entire building up to current building codes is mandatory, which includes compliance with the Americans with Disabilities Act (ADA). ADA compliance primarily involves ensuring barrier-free accessibility to and within the building, such as accessible entryways, ramps, parking, elevators, and restrooms. ADA improvements must provide clear, unobstructed paths and appropriately equipped facilities that accommodate individuals with disabilities. It's crucial to clearly determine and document whether ADA compliance responsibilities rest with the tenant or landlord, as costs can be significant—often exceeding $100,000 for even a single building. Planning and budgeting proactively can help manage these potential financial impacts.

Hazardous Material Handling & Storage (EPA compliance and legal risk mitigation)

Understanding what types of materials your tenants are storing and using on your property is critical to any sophisticated landlord. We recommend creating a written policy about how chemicals should be delivered, stored safely and disposed of. Then incorporate these best practices into your lease obligations to ensure that the tenant complies with these procedures. Requesting MSDS forms from a tenant will help shape the particular policies for a tenant and help your insurance broker understand what elevated risks you would face from an insurance policy premium perspective. Depending on the quantities involved, you may require a containment pad, overflow curbs and may also ban certain chemicals entirely. There is no right or wrong answer, but you must develop a policy as to your own risk tolerance for hazardous materials. This effort will pay dividends during the tenant's lease, during insurance renewals, and when convincing a buyer that your property is properly insulated from environmental risks.

While this chapter covers major legal issues for industrial investors ranging from acquisition, operations and disposition, the best investors that I work with understand that lawyers are just a tool. They are only as good as the clients who direct them. Therefore, smart investors continue to learn about legal updates, communicate frequently with legal counsel and continually update their internal policies over time.

29

Common Documents & Forms

IN INDUSTRIAL REAL ESTATE TRANSACTIONS, whether involving a sale or lease, negotiations traditionally begin with parties establishing alignment on essential business terms before advancing into comprehensive legal documentation. This preliminary stage is crucial, serving as the foundational framework upon which the entirety of the transaction is built. It provides clarity and mutual understanding of expectations, ensuring both parties are synchronized on the significant aspects before progressing to more detailed, legally-binding agreements.

For leases, this initial negotiation typically commences with a Letter of Intent (LOI). An LOI succinctly captures the transaction's critical business terms, such as rental rates, lease duration, renewal options, security deposits, tenant improvement allowances, and occupancy commencement dates. The LOI is pivotal as it helps both the landlord and tenant identify potential conflicts or misalignments early in the process, thereby reducing the risk of disputes as discussions evolve into formal lease agreements.

Similarly, purchase transactions usually begin with either an Offer to Purchase (OTP) or a detailed Term Sheet. These documents typically include essential items like the purchase price, earnest money deposits, due diligence periods, closing dates, financing contingencies, zoning approvals, environmental assessments, and any other unique terms relevant to the transaction. The OTP or Term Sheet acts as a blueprint, guiding subsequent due diligence and negotiations, providing transparency and reducing the possibility of misunderstandings or overlooked items.

While LOIs, OTPs, and Term Sheets are typically non-binding, they represent a clear and documented mutual understanding of the critical business terms and serve as a guiding document for drafting the formal contracts. These documents often explicitly state their non-binding nature, except for specific provisions like confidentiality or exclusivity, which the parties may agree are binding.

Employing these preliminary documents significantly streamlines the negotiation process. By highlighting deal-breakers and aligning on critical business terms upfront, parties save considerable time and reduce legal costs. This early stage allows for transparent and open communication, fostering a collaborative environment where objectives can be clearly stated, concessions openly discussed, and mutual trust established prior to involving legal representatives for final drafting and execution of definitive agreements.

Beyond the LOI, OTP, and Term Sheet, several other common documents and forms play crucial roles in industrial real estate transactions.

These may include:

Non-Disclosure Agreement (NDA): Used to protect sensitive business information shared between parties during negotiations.

Estoppel Certificate: A document where the tenant confirms key lease terms to the prospective buyer or lender, thereby limiting future disputes.

Assignment and Assumption Agreements: Used when leases or contracts are transferred from one party to another during a transaction.

Subordination, Non-Disturbance, and Attornment Agreement (SNDA): Ensures tenants' rights under leases are clearly defined in relation to a lender's interests, protecting both lender and tenant interests during financing.

Lease Abstract: A concise summary highlighting the critical terms and conditions of a lease agreement. Typically used by landlords, tenants, property managers, brokers, and attorneys, a lease abstract simplifies complex lease details such as rental obligations, lease commencement and expiration dates, renewal options, tenant improvement allowances, escalation clauses, operating expense responsibilities, and other essential provisions. This document serves as a quick-reference tool, streamlining lease administration, financial analysis, due diligence, and strategic decision-making.

Rent Roll: A comprehensive document summarizing key information about tenants within a commercial property, including tenant names, occupied suite numbers, leased areas, rental rates, lease commencement and expiration dates, security deposits, renewal options, and additional notes relevant to the lease terms. Rent rolls are vital tools used by landlords, investors, property managers, and brokers to efficiently manage properties, conduct financial analysis, track lease expirations, assess tenant risk profiles, and evaluate overall property performance.

Incorporating these documents strategically at appropriate stages ensures comprehensive risk mitigation and efficient transactional flow. Parties become equipped to proactively identify and address potential issues, reducing the risk of costly delays or litigation post-closing.

A simple Letter of Intent (LOI) & Offer to Purchase (OTP) can be downloaded for free by visiting:
https://industrialize.com/forms-and-templates

It is imperative to emphasize the importance of obtaining professional legal advice at all stages of negotiation and document preparation. Even preliminary documents like LOIs and OTPs can contain nuanced provisions that have significant implications. Professional legal counsel can ensure the transaction structure accurately reflects the parties' intentions and legal protections are appropriately in place.

Summary

Clearly structured and carefully prepared preliminary documents establish a strong foundation, promote transparency, build trust, and enable smoother, more predictable transitions into formal contractual agreements. They are essential tools in the industrial real estate professional's toolkit, critical for effectively navigating complex transactions.

30

Tenant Improvements (TIs)

TENANT IMPROVEMENTS (TIs) are modifications made to an industrial property to meet the specific needs of a tenant. These modifications can range from minor upgrades like new lighting and flooring to major structural changes such as adding mezzanines, dock doors, or specialized HVAC systems.

Tenant improvements play a key role in lease negotiations, often determining who pays for what, how costs are allocated, and how improvements impact lease length and rental rates.

This chapter explores common TIs, cost considerations, lease structuring, and how different industrial asset classes approach improvements.

Expert Insight:

"Industrial real estate has low capital expenditures, low ongoing maintenance, and stable cash flow. I'd much rather own warehouses with CPI increases every year than an office building where significant tenant improvements are needed every time a tenant leaves."
—Walk Rakowich, Former CEO of Prologis

Although Tenant Improvements may be less than other asset classes, it's important to identify what may be required.

Common Types of Tenant Improvements

The scope of TIs depends on the industry, property type, and lease agreement. Some tenants require basic modifications, while others need extensive upgrades to operate efficiently.

Common Tenant Improvements

- Lighting upgrades: LED conversions, high-bay fixtures for warehouses.
- Painting & basic flooring – Epoxy coatings, polished concrete, or basic carpet for office space.
- Office buildouts: Standard office spaces inside warehouses or manufacturing facilities.
- HVAC servicing: Ensuring systems are in working condition at lease commencement.
- Dock door adjustment: Seals, bumpers, or minor modifications to accommodate tenant logistics.

Custom Tenant Improvements (Tenant-Specific)

These modifications are tailored to a tenant's operations and often require landlord approval before construction. There is a virtually endless number of potential upgrades, but here are a few examples:

- Electrical Upgrades: Voltage increases, additional panels
- Heavy-Duty Flooring – Reinforced slabs for heavy machinery or vibration-dampening solutions.
- Specialized HVAC Systems – Climate control for cold storage or Make Up Air systems
- Overhead Cranes & Racking Systems – Structural reinforcements to support equipment.
- Loading Dock Modifications – Additional dock-high doors, dock levellers, drive-in ramps, or cross-dock configurations.
- Mezzanine Construction – Adding second-level office space or storage platforms.

Industry-Specific Tenant Improvements

Some industries require highly specialized improvements that go beyond standard buildouts:

- Cold Storage Facilities: Insulated walls, freezer/cooler panels, industrial refrigeration systems.
- Biotech & Pharmaceutical Labs: Cleanrooms, fume hoods, deionized water systems.

- TechFlex & Data Centers: High-capacity power systems, backup generators, fiber optics.
- Manufacturing Plants: Reinforced foundations, crane systems, heavy exhaust systems, specialized fire suppression.

Best Practice

Before signing a lease, tenants should work with contractors, engineers, and city planners to determine feasibility, permitting, and timeline for required improvements.

Who Pays for Tenant Improvements?

The responsibility for funding tenant improvements (TIs) varies widely, depending on lease negotiations, property type, market conditions, and tenant requirements. Typically, tenant improvements are structured into one of three primary arrangements:

Landlord-Funded Improvements (TI Allowance)
In this arrangement, the landlord provides the tenant with a predetermined dollar amount per square foot to be used toward specific improvements. The tenant typically manages the construction process, but the landlord reimburses costs up to the agreed-upon allowance limit. If the allowance is not fully utilized, the remaining funds may revert to the landlord unless the tenant negotiates an alternative arrangement, such as applying leftover funds toward rent credits or other operational expenses.

For instance, consider a warehouse lease that includes a TI allowance of $5.00 per square foot. This allowance enables the tenant to enhance lighting systems and expand office areas without incurring significant out-of-pocket expenses.

Tenant-Funded Improvements
In cases where the tenant has highly specialized or industry-specific needs—such as heavy manufacturing, research and development, or laboratory facilities—the tenant typically bears the full cost of improvements. The tenant then retains ownership of removable modifications, granting them flexibility to relocate or reuse specialized equipment after the lease ends.

For example, a biotechnology company investing $2 million into laboratory upgrades may structure their lease to ensure that equipment and specialized infrastructure remain their property, allowing them to remove and relocate their investment upon lease expiration. This arrangement often provides tenants with increased leverage during lease negotiations, potentially enabling them to secure rent reductions or other favorable lease terms.

Landlord-Built Improvements (Turnkey Buildout)
Under a turnkey arrangement, the landlord takes responsibility for designing, constructing, and delivering a fully move-in ready space. This option is common in new developments or build-to-suit properties and is usually favored in long-term leases ranging from 5 to 10 or more years. In such cases, improvement costs are typically amortized into the rent over the lease period.

As an example, a logistics firm signing a 10-year lease might require specialized infrastructure such as cross-docking facilities, advanced racking systems, and conveyor technology. The landlord, under a turnkey agreement, would manage the entire construction process and deliver a fully equipped facility upon the lease commencement.

Key Lease Considerations for Tenant Improvements

Amortization of TIs: When landlords finance improvements beyond standard allowances, they commonly seek to recover these costs through amortization built into the rental payments. This means the landlord calculates the cost of improvements, applies an agreed-upon interest rate, and spreads the total expense over the lease term.

For example, if a landlord of a 12,000 square foot space provides a $200,000 tenant improvement package beyond the standard allowance and amortizes this cost over five years at a 7% interest rate, it would add approximately $4.00 per square foot annually to the base rent.

Both landlords and tenants should clearly document these amortization terms within the lease to ensure transparency and avoid future disputes.

Annual Payment Calculation for the above example:

Using a standard amortization formula (annual payment = principal ×

amortization factor):

Annual Payment=$200,000×0.2439=$48,780
(Note: The factor 0.2439 is from standard amortization tables for a 5-year term at 7%)

Cost per Square Foot (assuming a 12,000 square-foot space):
$48,780 / 12,000 sq. ft. = $4.07 / sq ft.
(rounded above to $4.00 / sq ft.)

Removal of Improvements at Lease Expiration

One critical consideration when negotiating Tenant Improvements (TIs) is determining their status at the end of the lease term. It's essential to address clearly whether the installed improvements are considered permanent fixtures or if they must be removed upon lease expiration.

Key questions to clarify include:

- Are the improvements permanent or removable?

  Clearly define in the lease which TIs are considered permanent fixtures (which remain landlord property), and which are removable by the tenant. For example, specialized equipment, overhead cranes, HVAC upgrades, lighting systems, or structural enhancements typically require specific consideration.
- Who bears the cost of restoration?

  If the lease stipulates that the tenant must remove improvements, it often also requires restoration of the property to its original condition. The costs associated with this can be significant and may involve repairing floors, walls, ceilings, and electrical or plumbing systems to their initial state. Both parties should carefully negotiate and document who is responsible for these costs.
- Will the landlord retain certain improvements?

In some cases, landlords may benefit from retaining improvements, particularly if they enhance the value or marketability of the property to future tenants. If the landlord opts to retain these improvements, tenants might negotiate reduced restoration responsibilities, lowering their lease-end obligations.

Case Study:

A manufacturing tenant installs reinforced flooring and overhead cranes tailored to their heavy manufacturing process. If the lease explicitly requires the tenant to remove these improvements and restore the facility at the end of the lease, the removal and restoration costs could easily exceed $100,000. Conversely, if the landlord anticipates future tenants may have similar needs, retaining these improvements could save significant time and money for all parties involved.

To mitigate disputes and financial surprises, tenants and landlords should thoroughly document expectations and responsibilities regarding improvement removal and restoration before lease execution.

Permitting & Approval Process

Before beginning any Tenant Improvements (TIs), tenants must typically secure approval from the landlord to ensure all proposed modifications align with the property's standards and the landlord's long-term goals. It is equally important to confirm compliance with local zoning ordinances, building codes, and safety regulations. Failure to adhere to these requirements can lead to costly delays, potential fines, or mandated removal of non-compliant improvements.

Leases also frequently place explicit restrictions on modifications, particularly those involving exterior alterations, structural changes, or signage. Tenants should thoroughly review these restrictions and, if necessary, negotiate exceptions upfront to prevent future disputes or unexpected expenses.

Case Study: Tenant Improvements in Action

Consider a logistics company that leased a 100,000-square-foot industrial facility and required significant enhancements to tailor the space for its operations. The improvements included expanding the dock capacity by adding four additional loading docks, performing a comprehensive LED lighting retrofit to increase energy efficiency, and constructing 20,000 square feet of office space. This office area featured break rooms, conference rooms, individual offices, and extensive IT infrastructure.

The total cost for these improvements broke down as follows: dock modifications at $160,000, the lighting retrofit at $250,000, and the office buildout amounting to $1,500,000, culminating in an overall investment of $1,910,000.

During lease negotiations, the landlord agreed to provide a Tenant Improvement allowance of $10 per square foot, totaling $1,000,000. The tenant was responsible for funding the remaining balance of $910,000.

This scenario highlights the highly customizable nature of TI negotiations, underscoring the dynamic and complex nature of industrial real estate transactions.

Summary

Tenant Improvements significantly influence lease negotiations. Clearly defining cost responsibilities, approval processes, and end-of-lease considerations is critical. Typically, landlords prefer longer leases to justify substantial TI allowances by spreading the investment over an extended period. Tenants, conversely, should be mindful of potential requirements to restore or remove improvements at lease expiration. Industry-specific enhancements demand meticulous planning to ensure compliance with zoning and permitting regulations and maintain long-term adaptability of the property.

31

Reports and Due Diligence

EFFECTIVE DUE DILIGENCE is the cornerstone of successful industrial real estate investments. It minimizes risks, ensures compliance, and provides a clearer understanding of the property's true condition and value. However, many investors, especially new ones, often underestimate the time, cost, and complexity involved in the process. This chapter breaks down the essential reports and considerations for comprehensive due diligence.

Environmental Site Assessment (ESA)

Phase I ESA: A non-invasive assessment that reviews the historical and current uses of the property to identify potential environmental risks. Includes historical records search, visual inspection, and interviews.

- Typical Cost and Timeline: $2,000 - $5,000 and 2-6 weeks.
- Outcome: Determines if further testing is recommended.

Phase II ESA: Involves soil, groundwater, and other subsurface testing to identify contamination. Includes sampling, laboratory analysis, and reporting.

- Typical Cost and Timeline: $10,000 - $50,000 or more and 4-8 weeks.
- Outcome: Identifies environmental remediation needs, if any.

Just a pet peeve of mine, but there is no such thing as a "clean" environmental report. It's an informal – and potentially reckless – way of describing a report that found no recognized environmental conditions (RECs). While this often means that no further investigation or remediation is required, an ESA does not guarantee the site is free from all environmental concerns. It simply means no issues were detected based on the scope of the assessment.

Property Condition Report / Building Condition Assessment)

A Property Condition Report (PCR) / Building Condition Assessment (BCA) evaluates the physical condition of the property's systems and structures and includes a breakdown on the roofing and structural integrity, HVAC, electrical, and plumbing systems, parking lots and drainage systems.

- Typical Cost and Timeline: $3,000 - $8,000 and 2-4 weeks.
- Outcome: Helps forecast repair and maintenance costs.

Appraisal

An appraisal determines the market value of the property and includes a comparable sales analysis, income approach and replacement cost analysis.

- Typical Cost and Timeline: $2,000 - $10,000 and 2-4 weeks.
- Outcome: Essential for lender underwriting and investment decision-making.

Geotechnical Report

A geotechnical report assesses soil conditions for structural stability and potential construction challenges. It won't likely be required for existing buildings but is generally needed for land or if a new building is being constructed. It includes borehole drilling and soil testing to analyze soil bearing capacity and drainage.

- Typical Cost and Timeline: $5,000 - $15,000 and 3-6 weeks.
- Outcome: Identifies potential foundation issues or construction constraints.

Component-Specific Reports

Many property owners get routine reports on specific components of the building and current reports can also be helpful if the owner is considering selling. Here are a couple common reports:

- Roofing Inspection: Assesses the condition, expected lifespan, and replacement costs.
- Mechanical System Reports: Evaluates HVAC, electrical, plumbing, or other critical systems.

Survey with Compliance Review

A survey (which may go by other names in different jurisdictions, such as a real property report) confirms property boundaries, easements, and compliance with zoning and building codes. These reports include boundary surveys, title surveys, and compliance verification.

- Typical Cost and Timeline: $2,000 - $6,000 and 2-4 weeks.
- Outcome: Identifies encroachments, zoning violations, or title discrepancies.

Legal Review and Searches

It is wise to hire an attorney to identify any potential risks. Services vary but generally include a title review, search for liens, encumbrances, or pending litigation and a review of leases, easements, and service agreements.

- Typical Cost and Timeline: $1,500 - $10,000 and 1-4 weeks.

Challenges in Due Diligence

Lender Requirements:

- Lenders may not accept reports commissioned by the seller.
- Reports often need updates or reassignment to include the buyer as the beneficiary.
- Vendors must be approved by the lender, necessitating new reports in some cases.

Market Variability:

Costs and timelines for reports fluctuate based on market conditions and busy markets may extend timelines by 2-4 weeks and increase costs by $5,000 or more.

Best Practices for Due Diligence

- Engage qualified professionals / hire third-party consultants for unbiased assessments.
- Use reputable national or regional firms for consistency and lender approval or confirm with your lender that your preferred consultant would be acceptable.
- Include sufficient time in the purchase agreement to complete due diligence.
- Budget for unexpected expenses, such as additional testing or repairs.
- Verify the validity and relevance of any existing reports.
- Confirm if they meet lender requirements or need updates.
- Address known issues immediately to avoid delays in closing.
- Keep lenders, legal counsel, brokers and consultants informed throughout the process.
- Coordinate timelines to ensure a smooth flow of information and decision-making.

Expert Insight

"Due diligence is all about risk management. It's not just checking boxes; it's making sure you fully understand what you're buying, financing, or leasing. People often underestimate the importance of clearly defining their objectives upfront. Your consultant should understand your goals because due diligence isn't just an expense—it's protection against costly surprises later."
—Jim Bartlett, Senior Vice President at Bureau Veritas

Summary

Conducting thorough due diligence is a time-intensive and costly process but is vital for mitigating risks and ensuring the success of an industrial real estate investment. From environmental assessments to property condition reports, each component plays a crucial role in providing a complete picture of the property's condition and value. By engaging qualified professionals, planning for contingencies, and maintaining clear communication, investors can navigate the complexities of due diligence and make informed decisions that support long-term success.

32

Financing

SECURING FINANCING for industrial real estate investments can be one of the most complex and nuanced aspects of the acquisition process. Whether you're purchasing a manufacturing facility, a warehouse, or a flex property, understanding the various financing options, structures, and key considerations is essential to ensuring a successful transaction. This chapter explores the common financing options.

Conventional Loans

Traditional loans provided by banks and financial institutions.

- Typically require a 20%-35% down payment.
- Fixed or variable interest rates.
- Terms ranging from 5 to 25 years.

Advantages of conventional loans include competitive interest rates and long terms and amortizations. Disadvantages include lengthy approval processes and strict underwriting criteria.

SBA Loans (U.S.)

Loans backed by the U.S. Small Business Administration (SBA), designed to support small businesses. (Note: there are similar types of loans available in Canada. Consult a mortgage broker to learn more).

- SBA 7(a): Flexible loan program for purchasing or renovating industrial properties.
- SBA 504: Specifically for purchasing fixed assets like real estate or large equipment.

Advantages include lower down payments and competitive interest rates while the disadvantages are a lengthy application process and potential restrictions on the property use.

CMBS Loans (Commercial Mortgage-Backed Securities)

Loans that are pooled together with other loans and sold to investors as securities. These loans are generally non-recourse (borrower's liability is limited to the property), have fixed interest rates and typically a balloon payment at the end of the term.

Advantages are competitive rates and easier approval process (particularly for experienced investors). Disadvantages include a lack of flexibility if you need to refinance or sell the property and a complex servicing structure. There may also be significant prepayment penalties due to yield maintenance clauses.

Private Financing

Loans from private investors or lending groups. These loans often have higher interest rates and shorter terms compared to conventional loans. The terms are negotiated directly with the lender and tend to be more flexible.

Advantages can include a faster approval process and flexible underwriting criteria, whereas the disadvantages are higher costs and limited scalability for larger projects.

Bridge Loans

Short-term financing used to "bridge" the gap until long-term financing is secured. These loans are generally shorter term (3 years or less) and have high interest rates and additional fees.

The advantage is quick access to capital, which can be useful for properties requiring renovations or lease stabilization. However, the loans are often expensive compared to other options and there's a risk of default if long-term / permanent financing isn't secured on time.

Seller Financing

The seller acts as the lender, allowing the buyer to make payments over time. The terms tend to be more flexible than conventional financing as its negotiated directly with the seller. These types of loans are often used when other loans aren't available (such as in a higher interest rate environment) or when a quicker closing process is needed. These types of loans can also be helpful in unique property situations.

Advantages include the ability to bypass traditional lenders and tailor the agreement to both buyer and seller needs. Disadvantages are that these loans often involve higher interest rates and are limited to the seller's willingness and capacity.

Interest Rates and Terms

- Fixed vs. Variable: Fixed rates provide stability, while variable rates may offer lower initial costs but can fluctuate.
- Balloon Payments: Understand the risks of loans with large payments due at the end of the term.
- Prepayment Penalties: Some loans include penalties for early repayment.

Loan-to-Value Ratio (LTV): Represents the ratio of the loan amount to the property's value. Most lenders require an LTV of 65%-80% for industrial properties.

Debt Service Coverage Ratio (DSCR): Lenders use this ratio to assess a property's ability to cover debt payments. The formula is as follows:

$$DSCR = \left(\frac{NOI}{Debt\ Service} \right)$$

Where   NOI = Net Operating Income, and
Debt Service = annual mortgage payments.

A DSCR of 1.20 to 1.25 (or higher) is typically required. Here is an example assuming a property has a Net Operating Income of $100,000 and annual debt payments of $80,000:

$$DSCR = \left(\frac{100,000}{80,000} \right) = 1.25$$

As part of the underwriting process, lenders look at two distinct elements of any potential loan: the borrower and the property.

Borrower Evaluation

- Creditworthiness: A strong credit score demonstrates a history of responsible borrowing and repayment.
- Credit History: Lenders look for a clean history without significant delinquencies, defaults, or bankruptcies.
- Net Worth: Ensures the borrower has sufficient assets to support the loan.
- Liquidity: Banks assess cash reserves or other liquid assets to cover unexpected expenses or shortfalls.
- Debt-to-Income Ratio: Ensures the borrower's overall debt obligations are manageable compared to income.
- Track Record: Experience in owning, managing, or developing industrial properties can be a critical factor.
- Industry Knowledge: Lenders prefer borrowers with a demonstrated understanding of industrial property operations and market conditions.
- Personal Guarantee: Lenders may require a personal guarantee, particularly for smaller borrowers or riskier loans, to ensure personal liability in case of default.
- Corporate Guarantee: If the company is buying the property lenders may also want a corporate guarantee.

Property Evaluation

Lenders want to fully understand the asset as a default by the borrower could mean the asset falls to the ownership of the lender. This includes property details, market analysis, income projections, and a clear strategy for repayment. The following reports are also generally required:

- Environmental Site Assessments (Phase I, and II, if necessary).
- Appraisal.
- Property Condition Report.

Even if financing is not required, prudent purchasers will want to understand potential risks and these reports can identify many of them. I would also recommend creating a detailed business plan that includes the information above in addition to contingency plans for any unexpected costs or setbacks.

Summary

Financing industrial real estate requires a thorough understanding of available options, lender expectations, and market conditions. By exploring conventional loans, SBA programs, CMBS loans, and other financing methods, investors can align their strategies with property-specific needs. Careful planning, strong financials, and proactive communication with lenders are essential to securing favorable terms and successfully closing deals.

33

Risks and Potential Pitfalls

INVESTING IN INDUSTRIAL real estate can be highly rewarding, but like any investment, it carries risks and potential pitfalls that require careful management. In this chapter, we'll explore common risks, mitigation strategies, and best practices to safeguard your investment.

Tenant-Related Risks

Tenants are integral to the value and success of industrial real estate, but they also introduce various operational risks. Industries such as heavy manufacturing, waste management, or hazardous materials storage inherently pose greater potential for property damage, environmental contamination, and regulatory issues. Properties heavily customized for specific tenants often necessitate costly and time-consuming modifications upon tenant turnover, impacting marketability, rental income, and overall property valuation.

Operational factors, including heavy machinery usage, chemical processes, noise, odors, or significant traffic, can accelerate wear and tear on critical infrastructure such as parking lots, loading docks, and interior building components. Additionally, tenants handling flammable or hazardous materials can trigger increased insurance premiums, void coverage, or even cause conflicts with neighboring tenants or local regulatory authorities. Changes of use or tenant turnover, even within similar industrial categories, frequently entail challenges related to zoning compatibility, adjustments to insurance coverage, and requirements to add costly systems such as sprinklers or makeup air units.

Mitigation Strategies:

Effective management of tenant-related risks requires thorough tenant vetting, including credit and reference checks and comprehensive operational assessments. Clearly articulated lease agreements, incorporating specific clauses to regulate tenant behavior and activities, along with regular property inspections, can significantly mitigate potential liabilities. Landlords should also require tenants to carry adequate insurance, naming the landlord as an additional insured party. Prioritizing financially stable tenants and negotiating favorable, long-term leases further enhance stability and reduce turnover risks. Lastly, it is prudent to regularly analyze property value and adaptability under a potential vacancy scenario to better understand and mitigate financial exposure.

Expert Insight

"One of the reasons we love Class B industrial is that often the downside can actually be the upside. If a tenant vacates, that can be our catalyst to quickly mark rents to market and create value. The ability to mitigate risk and still find opportunities is what makes this space so compelling."
—Zach Harris and Hunt Rose from TruCore Investments

Environmental Risks

Industrial properties, especially older ones, frequently face environmental hazards such as asbestos, lead-based paint, and residual contamination from previous occupants. Soil or groundwater contamination poses financial, regulatory, and reputational risks, and remediation efforts can be costly. Additionally, tenants who generate emissions or dust may attract regulatory attention or complaints from the community.

Mitigation Strategies:

Conducting thorough Phase I and Phase II Environmental Site Assessments (ESA) during due diligence, incorporating environmental indemnity clauses in leases, and proactively monitoring for contamination can substantially reduce environmental risks. Engaging experienced environmental consultants helps ensure ongoing compliance with environmental regulations.

Legal and Regulatory Risks

Zoning regulations, building codes, and lease agreements present legal and regulatory challenges. Tenants using properties in non-compliant ways can trigger regulatory actions, fines, or operational shutdowns.

Older buildings often require upgrades to meet evolving building codes, presenting unexpected costs. Additionally, ambiguously drafted leases expose landlords to costly disputes or collection issues.

Mitigation Strategies:

Engaging seasoned real estate attorneys to draft robust lease agreements, regularly updating knowledge of zoning laws, and conducting property condition assessments to ensure compliance proactively reduce legal and regulatory exposures.

Financial Risks

Extended vacancies and economic fluctuations can drastically impact revenue and profitability. Rising property taxes, insurance premiums, and maintenance costs compound these challenges, potentially eroding profitability and property values.

Mitigation Strategies:

Maintaining diversified tenant bases, establishing reserve funds, continuously monitoring market conditions, and employing triple-net (NNN) leases to offset operational costs are effective strategies for mitigating financial risks.

Expert Insight

"In 2008, I had 50 buildings, seven banks, and 63 people I had borrowed from. I was so deep into debt that I nearly lost everything. I came to the conclusion that I needed to go back to my roots—doing all-cash, no mortgages, so that I could sleep at night."
—Joel Friedland, co-founder of Brit Properties.

Property Condition Risks

Deferred maintenance, particularly of roofs, concrete floors, and parking lots, can rapidly escalate into significant expenditures. Poor drainage and general wear-and-tear can magnify these issues.

Mitigation Strategies:

Conducting regular, detailed inspections, prioritizing preventative maintenance, budgeting for capital expenditures, and utilizing professional structural assessments safeguard against unexpected large-scale repairs.

Natural Disaster Risks

Properties exposed to flooding, seismic activity, hurricanes, tornadoes, or other natural disasters face structural risks and operational interruptions that can severely impact businesses.

Mitigation Strategies:

Acquiring suitable insurance, retrofitting properties to local disaster-resilience standards, and developing comprehensive emergency preparedness plans protect assets and tenant safety.

Unknown Risks

Real estate investments inevitably involve unforeseen risks. Despite thorough preparation, unanticipated events or market changes can still occur.

Mitigation Strategies:

Accepting risks, seeking advice from trusted advisors, and stress-testing investments by considering worst-case scenarios help manage uncertainty effectively. Networking and sharing insights with industry peers also provide valuable perspectives that can identify overlooked risks.

Case Study

An investor purchased a freestanding industrial building leased to a reputable construction company in a small market near a large city. Two years into the purchase, the tenant vacated despite having four years left on the lease, continuing to pay rent but failing to sublease the property. When the lease ended, the owner similarly struggled to find tenants due to low ceilings, inadequate loading, limited power, and market size limitations. Ultimately, the property went into receivership.

Key Lesson: Treat every investment opportunity as if fully vacant. Analyze the building comprehensively, considering all potential negatives and market limitations. Ask critical questions such as:

- Can identified issues be economically remedied?
- How long might re-leasing realistically take?
- What financial exposure results from potentially lower market rents?
- What is the worst-case scenario, including foreclosure or receivership?
- Knowing these risks, is the investment still attractive?
- Had this investor completed such an analysis, he likely would have identified the property's inherent limitations and reconsidered the investment.

Summary

Protecting downside risk is essential in industrial real estate investing. Investors should always evaluate properties as if vacant, regardless of current occupancy status, to identify hidden risks and accurately assess investment potential. Proactive strategies—including diligent tenant selection, regular property assessments, compliance with regulations, and planning for unforeseen contingencies—form the backbone of successful long-term industrial real estate investments.

34

Additional Considerations

INDUSTRIAL REAL ESTATE is a dynamic and ever-evolving sector, requiring stakeholders to account for a variety of additional considerations beyond the standard factors of location, size, and tenant mix. This chapter dives into emerging trends, evolving business practices, and forward-looking concepts that are shaping the future of industrial real estate.

Expert Insight

"Real estate investing isn't about projecting trends perfectly—it's about being prepared, nimble, and disciplined enough to respond when opportunities arise. Always protect your downside, stay flexible, and challenge assumptions. The best investors aren't necessarily the ones who predict the future—they're the ones who adapt effectively to the present."
– Michael Golden, President and CEO of Gladstone

Growing Power Demands

As industrial operations evolve, the demand for electricity continues to rise sharply. Automation, robotics, electric vehicle (EV) charging, and energy-intensive machinery all contribute significantly to increased electrical loads. Older properties, often built with limited electrical capacity, face substantial hurdles in adapting to these new requirements. Upgrading such facilities can be prohibitively expensive or structurally challenging.

In response, modern developments are being designed proactively to include enhanced electrical infrastructure, additional conduit for future upgrades, and dedicated spaces for EV charging and renewable energy integration. This forward-thinking approach helps buildings remain competitive, making them attractive to tenants looking for long-term operational efficiency and flexibility.

Supply Chain Strategies: Just-in-Time vs. Just-in-Case

The supply chain disruptions caused by global events, notably the recent pandemic, exposed the vulnerabilities of just-in-time (JIT) inventory models, prompting a shift towards just-in-case (JIC) strategies. JIC models prioritize inventory resilience, driving the need for increased warehouse space, enhanced logistics capabilities, and flexible building designs to accommodate larger inventories and diversified supplier bases.

Industrial properties capable of adapting quickly to changes in storage requirements, dock configurations, and advanced logistics technologies will see significant advantages. The ability to seamlessly switch between JIT and JIC practices ensures properties remain highly desirable in fluctuating market conditions.

Additive Manufacturing / Print-on-Demand

The growth of additive manufacturing (3D printing) promises a profound impact on industrial real estate. This technology enables localized, on-demand production, reducing the need for large, centralized manufacturing facilities and expansive warehousing. Companies adopting additive manufacturing often seek smaller, technologically advanced spaces equipped to handle specialized equipment, robust electrical supply, and enhanced digital connectivity.

However, adoption barriers such as high upfront costs, skilled labor requirements, and material limitations remain. Properties that can address these demands effectively will be best positioned to capitalize on this transformative trend.

War Production

Industrial real estate has historically been closely tied to war production. Today's geopolitical landscape continues this tradition, driving demand for facilities capable of manufacturing defense equipment, precision engineering components, and advanced weaponry. Facilities specializing in aerospace, heavy manufacturing, and logistics become critical infrastructure, supported by robust supply chains and secure locations.

Increased investment in defense infrastructure further underscores the strategic importance of industrial real estate. Properties close to transportation corridors or military installations gain strategic significance, attracting long-term interest from government and defense contractors.

Autonomous Delivery Vehicles & Drones

Autonomous vehicles and drones are transforming logistics, particularly in middle-mile and last-mile deliveries. Autonomous trucks used for middle-mile transport require properties strategically located near major highways, while drone-based last-mile deliveries favor urban micro-fulfillment centers with dedicated drone launch facilities and specialized docking stations.

This technological shift demands facilities designed to accommodate automation infrastructure, advanced power systems, and innovative space utilization, significantly influencing property values and market demand.

Automation and Cubic Storage

Automation technologies, including automated guided vehicles (AGVs) and retrieval systems, are redefining warehouse efficiency. Facilities now prioritize superflat floors, high connectivity, and vertical storage solutions to optimize cubic space utilization. Rising clear heights—now frequently exceeding 40 feet—allow for multi-tier racking systems, significantly enhancing storage capacity.

Despite the benefits, high initial capital requirements and regulatory hurdles may slow widespread adoption. Nonetheless, properties designed to support automation and vertical storage solutions will enjoy competitive advantages and higher tenant appeal.

Energy Efficiency and Solar Readiness

Energy efficiency and renewable energy integration, particularly solar, have become critical considerations. Solar-ready designs, energy-efficient lighting, and advanced HVAC systems are now essential features that increase property attractiveness, lower operational costs, and mitigate risks associated with future power shortages.

Such features not only improve market value but also align with governmental incentives and sustainability goals, further enhancing property desirability and financial performance.

Smart Technologies

The integration of smart technologies, including IoT systems, automated building management, and predictive maintenance, is increasingly important. These technologies improve operational efficiency, reduce costs, and enhance tenant satisfaction by offering real-time monitoring and proactive management of property assets.

Dark Warehouses

Fully automated "dark" warehouses represent the cutting edge of logistics, featuring minimal human intervention and maximum operational efficiency. By leveraging robotics, AI, and automation, dark warehouses optimize space utilization, reduce operational costs, and offer unparalleled inventory management capabilities.

Although initial investments are significant, the operational savings and enhanced efficiency position these facilities as crucial components in the future logistics landscape. Properties able to support such advanced automation systems will become increasingly valuable.

Office Space in Industrial Buildings

The evolving office space needs within industrial properties, accelerated by hybrid work trends, require flexible design solutions. Modular office spaces that adapt easily to changing tenant requirements are increasingly important. Properties offering adjustable layouts and efficient space use will cater effectively to varying office demands.

Monitoring & Regular Inspections

Proactive monitoring and inspections safeguard property longevity and operational reliability. Advanced security systems, environmental sensors, and regular inspections mitigate risks such as vandalism, structural damage, or utility disruptions, maintaining tenant satisfaction and property integrity.

Expert Insight

"If you're not continually maintaining a building, it's degrading, and that degradation accelerates over time."
—Don Catalano, President of iOptimize Realty.

Case Study

Two years ago, on Christmas Day, a water pipe burst inside an industrial building I own. Of course, it had to happen on the one day of the year when the building was completely unoccupied — no tenants, no staff, not even a passerby to hear the water running. The leak went unnoticed for over 24 hours, allowing thousands of gallons to seep into the space undisturbed. By the time it was discovered, it had already soaked through multiple offices, damaging drywall, warping flooring, and destroying desks, chairs, computers, and other furniture.

What started as a simple, silent rupture turned into a multi-month ordeal. The remediation process alone — water extraction, mold prevention, and demolition of affected materials — took weeks. Rebuilding took even longer, as crews had to replace not only structural components but also coordinate with electricians, flooring contractors, and commercial furniture suppliers. Tenants were displaced, operations were interrupted, and insurance claims became their own full-time job.

In total, the damage exceeded several hundred thousand dollars, and the ripple effects were felt well beyond just the physical repairs. It served as a brutal reminder that in industrial real estate, even one day of vulnerability can turn into months of inconvenience, and a relatively minor component — like a pipe — can carry major consequences when left unchecked.

Summary

The future of industrial real estate hinges on adaptability to technological advancements, evolving tenant requirements, and sustainability initiatives. Stakeholders that proactively embrace automation, energy efficiency, smart technologies, and flexible design will thrive, maintaining competitive advantages in an increasingly sophisticated and demanding market.

35

Tools and Platforms

NAVIGATING THE INDUSTRIAL real estate market requires access to the right tools, platforms, and resources. This chapter provides a comprehensive guide to the most valuable tools and strategies that can help readers stay informed, make data-driven decisions, and streamline their operations.

Another important note: too many people rely on market-wide statistics when making decisions. There is a BIG difference between lease rates on a 200,000 sq ft distribution center and a 20,000 sq ft manufacturing facility on 5 acres of land.

To ensure you are comparing apples-to-apples, here are a few resources that could help:

Online Listing Platforms

Unlike the residential market, the industrial real estate market is less centralized, with information often scattered across multiple sources. However, the following platforms provide valuable starting points:

- LoopNet: One of the largest commercial real estate listing platforms, offering extensive industrial property listings across North America.
- Crexi: A user-friendly platform for buying, selling, and leasing commercial real estate, including industrial properties.
- CoStar: A premium platform providing in-depth market data, analytics, and property listings.
- Local Commercial MLS Systems: Many cities and regions have their own multiple listing services (MLS) for commercial properties. These can be excellent resources for localized information.

Market Research Tools

Understanding market trends is essential for making informed decisions. Here are tools that can provide critical insights:

- The Linneman Letter by Dr. Peter Linneman
- CBRE Market Reports: Comprehensive quarterly and annual reports on industrial real estate trends, including vacancy rates, lease rates, and construction pipelines.
- JLL Industrial Market Insights: Provides global and regional analysis of industrial markets, focusing on logistics, e-commerce, and supply chain dynamics.
- Savills Research: Offers detailed reports on industrial and logistics property markets worldwide, including emerging trends and investment opportunities.
- Cushman & Wakefield Reports: In-depth market research and forecasting for industrial properties, with a focus on local and global trends.
- Colliers International Insights: Features industrial real estate updates, market statistics, and investment opportunities across key regions.
- Marcus & Millichap Research Services: Provides comprehensive market reports tailored to investors, focusing on regional and national industrial trends.
- Avison Young Market Research: Regularly publishes insights on industrial real estate, including emerging opportunities and market performance.
- Prologis Research: Industry-specific research on logistics and supply chain impacts, often with a focus on warehouse demand and e-commerce growth.
- Newmark Knight Frank Reports: Offers market intelligence on industrial real estate trends, investment strategies, and tenant requirements.
- Real Capital Analytics (RCA): Tracks commercial property transactions and provides detailed analytics for industrial real estate investment.
- Federal Reserve Economic Data (FRED): Tracks macro-economic indicators, such as manufacturing output and freight transportation, that impact industrial real estate demand.

Networking and Industry Organizations

Building relationships within the industry is crucial for accessing off-market opportunities and staying ahead of trends. Consider joining these organizations:

- NAIOP (Commercial Real Estate Development Association): Offers networking events, educational resources, and market insights specific to industrial and commercial real estate.
- SIOR (Society of Industrial and Office Realtors): A professional organization for brokers specializing in industrial and office real estate, providing access to exclusive listings and market data.
- ULI (Urban Land Institute): Focuses on sustainable development and urban planning, offering valuable insights for industrial investors.
- Local Chambers of Commerce: Connect with local businesses and gain insights into regional economic trends that impact industrial real estate.

Expert Insight

"Real estate is a relationship business. Those who treated their clients well during challenging times will be remembered. Those who took advantage will also be remembered. Your reputation isn't built when things are easy; it's defined by how you handle the tough times."
–Sandy Shindleman, CEO of Shindico

Technology and PropTech Tools

- PropTech solutions are transforming the way industrial real estate is managed, marketed, and analyzed. Consider leveraging the following tools:
- Reonomy: A property intelligence platform offering detailed ownership and property data. Useful for prospecting and understanding market dynamics.
- Buildout: A marketing and CRM platform designed for commercial real estate professionals. Simplifies the process of creating property brochures, email campaigns, and listing syndications.

- Matterport: Creates 3D virtual tours of industrial properties, enhancing online listings and providing potential tenants or buyers with an immersive experience.
- VTS: A leasing and asset management platform that helps landlords and brokers track deals, manage tenants, and analyze portfolio performance.

Expert Insight

"PropTech is really any application of technology that enhances any part of the real estate lifecycle—from transactions and pre-development to construction and property management. The lifecycle can span decades or even centuries, and technology has the power to influence every aspect of it."
—Derek Hsiang, The Proptech Scout

Staying Updated with Industry News

Keeping up with the latest developments in industrial real estate is essential. Here are some top resources:

- GlobeSt.com: A leading source for commercial real estate news, including industrial trends and transactions.
- Bisnow: Covers a wide range of commercial real estate topics, with a focus on market trends and major deals.
- Commercial Property Executive: Provides in-depth analysis and news on industrial real estate, including investment opportunities and market forecasts.
- Industrial Distribution Magazine: Focuses on supply chain and distribution trends, which directly impact industrial real estate demand.

Expert Insight

"Don't just be a passive spectator in commercial real estate. Become a student of the game. Read, learn, apply, and master your craft."
–Rod Santomassimo, President and Founder of the Massimo Group

Data and Analytics Tools

For investors and developers, access to accurate data is paramount. Here are some tools to consider:

- ESRI ArcGIS: A powerful mapping tool that provides spatial analysis for site selection, market analysis, and logistics planning.
- Placer.ai: Analyzes foot traffic and customer behavior patterns around industrial sites, offering insights into accessibility and demand.
- Moody's Analytics: Offers economic and market forecasting tools, helping investors anticipate changes in industrial demand.
- Dodge Data & Analytics: Tracks construction projects and trends, providing insights into new industrial developments.

AI and advanced data analytics tools can greatly assist in analyzing and interpreting the large amount of data in the industry. Readers should remain aware that these technologies may produce occasional inaccuracies, incomplete analyses, or outdated information. It's important to independently verify key findings and cross-reference critical data points before making investment or development decisions.

Expert Insight

"There's definitely a risk of over-reliance on AI. You still have to cross-check it, but the time it saves is immense, and the accuracy keeps improving."
— Mark Duclos, President of Sentry Commercial

Physical Tools

When visiting industrial properties, inspections, or construction sites, the following tools can be very helpful and may be mandatory in construction areas or when in active businesses.

- Laser Measurer: Quickly and accurately measure distances, heights, and spaces within buildings.
- Knife & Scissors: Essential for cutting materials or opening packages on-site.
- Flashlight: Useful for entering buildings that may have light switches or breakers away from the main door. Also, for inspecting poorly lit areas like electrical and mechanical rooms, or ceiling structures.
- Hard Hat: Required for safety in construction zones or areas with

potential overhead hazards.

- Steel Toe Boots: Protects feet in industrial environments, especially in warehouses or construction sites.
- Safety Vest: Ensures visibility when walking around active work zones or high-traffic areas.
- Safety Glasses: Protects eyes during inspections or when working in areas with flying debris.
- First Aid Kit: A crucial item for addressing minor injuries or emergencies during site visits.

Expert Insight

"You can't eat an elephant in one bite—success is about small, consistent action over time. Focus on taking one step at a time, and eventually you'll look back and be amazed by how far you've come."
– Rafael Collazo, CCIM, Commercial Real Estate Advisor

Summary

Navigating the industrial real estate market requires more than just a keen eye for properties; it demands comprehensive access to specialized tools, advanced platforms, and deep industry knowledge. Professionals in this dynamic sector benefit greatly from utilizing an array of online listing platforms, which facilitate immediate access to property availability, transaction history, and competitive market comparisons. Advanced market research tools allow users to analyze data such as demographic shifts, economic trends, and supply chain influences, enabling more strategic decision-making.

The rise of PropTech innovations has significantly transformed the industrial real estate landscape, bringing cutting-edge technology into traditional real estate practices. Tools such as virtual tours, 3D modeling, predictive analytics, and artificial intelligence enhance property assessments, streamline due diligence processes, and allow users to forecast market behaviors with greater accuracy and efficiency. These innovations not only speed up transactions but also reduce the inherent risks associated with investment and leasing activities.

Additionally, active participation in industry networks and professional platforms provides invaluable opportunities for knowledge exchange, relationship building, and gaining insights into emerging trends. Leveraging these networks can lead to partnerships, collaborative opportunities, and first-hand information on shifts occurring within local and global markets.

By effectively harnessing these diverse resources, readers will be better positioned to anticipate market movements, optimize their investment and leasing strategies, and seize opportunities that arise in the rapidly evolving industrial real estate sector.

36

Conclusion

AS WE'VE JOURNEYED through the chapters of this book, one truth stands out unmistakably: industrial real estate is a remarkably intricate and sophisticated field. Every decision—whether regarding ceiling heights, zoning compliance, loading configurations, or tenant improvements—plays a vital role in determining the property's functionality, desirability, and overall market value.

For some, industrial real estate conjures images of stark, unremarkable structures designed purely for utility. However, as we've explored together, these properties are fundamental drivers of global commerce. They continuously evolve to accommodate groundbreaking technologies, shifting market demands, and complex logistical necessities.

Successfully navigating industrial real estate requires precise attention to detail and an unyielding commitment to foresight. From ensuring optimal utilities and infrastructure to mastering tenant dynamics and regulatory landscapes, every factor deserves meticulous consideration. This industry rewards proactive individuals who not only adapt but anticipate future trends like automation, cutting-edge logistics, and technological breakthroughs.

Whether you're a seasoned investor, a professional broker, or someone just entering this fascinating domain, the insights, tools, and strategies shared throughout these chapters are designed to empower you to confidently face the challenges and seize the opportunities inherent in industrial real estate.

As you move forward, consider these key lessons:

Industrial Real Estate is Essential

It underpins modern commerce, providing critical spaces where goods are efficiently manufactured, stored, and distributed. Properties must precisely align with tenant needs, whether logistics hubs or specialized manufacturing facilities.

The Tenant is King

The primary purpose of industrial properties is to facilitate tenant operations. A property's true value is closely tied to tenant usability and the rent they are willing to pay. Tenant selection, therefore, becomes one of the most critical decisions an investor or landlord will ever make. A poorly chosen tenant can lead to financial instability, accelerated wear, and diminished property value, whereas the right tenant brings reliability, stable revenue, and enhanced long-term appreciation. Remember, industrial real estate is an active pursuit, requiring strategic management, relationship building, and ongoing responsiveness to tenant needs.

Manage Downside Risks First

In industrial real estate, managing risk should precede every decision. Attractive revenue projections can blind investors to the realities of market shifts, tenant volatility, or regulatory changes. Even seemingly minor details like insufficient clear heights or inadequate power capacity can derail a promising investment. Always perform comprehensive risk assessments before proceeding; this practice ensures long-term viability, protecting you from costly miscalculations.

Adaptability Drives Success

The industrial landscape continuously evolves, driven by innovations in automation, logistics technology, and emerging market dynamics. Embracing and preparing for advancements such as autonomous vehicles, drone logistics, and smart manufacturing can significantly enhance your competitive advantage. Remaining adaptable ensures you're not just keeping pace—you're leading the way.

Due Diligence is Non-Negotiable

Rigorous due diligence forms the foundation of every successful industrial real estate investment. Physical inspections, thorough environmental assessments, and detailed infrastructure evaluations can prevent costly future issues. Overlooking critical aspects—such as structural integrity, utility capacities, or potential environmental liabilities—can quickly turn profitable ventures into expensive nightmares.

Legal and financial scrutiny is equally vital. Carefully reviewing lease terms, zoning implications, title encumbrances, tenant financial stability, and projected operating costs reduces exposure to unforeseen complications. Investing time upfront in thorough diligence safeguards your financial outcomes and maximizes your returns.

Collaboration Unlocks Opportunity

No successful industrial real estate venture happens in isolation. It requires collaboration with an expert team comprising brokers, appraisers, attorneys, lenders, architects, engineers, and environmental specialists. Each professional brings indispensable expertise, helping you navigate the industry's multifaceted challenges and enhancing your decision-making processes.

Building and nurturing professional relationships—ranging from trusted contractors and municipal authorities to logistics experts—can streamline operations, reduce risks, and uncover hidden opportunities. Strategic collaboration invariably leads to better outcomes, cost efficiencies, and enhanced competitive positioning.

Prepare for the Unexpected

Despite thorough preparation, challenges will inevitably arise. Market fluctuations, unexpected maintenance issues, regulatory shifts, and economic changes can emerge without warning. Your ability to remain resilient, flexible, and solution-oriented when faced with these obstacles will ultimately define your long-term success.

Looking Ahead

Ultimately, industrial real estate transcends the simple concept of four walls and a roof. It embodies the heart of modern industry, connecting manufacturing, distribution, innovation, and global trade. It's about envisioning and preparing for the future of how goods are created, managed, and transported.

Next time someone underestimates industrial real estate, you'll recognize its true significance: a dynamic, foundational industry that supports thriving businesses, catalyzes innovation, and sustains economies worldwide.

Let this book be your ongoing guide, a reliable companion in your journey through industrial real estate. Thank you for embarking on this adventure, and may your endeavors in this compelling, ever-evolving industry lead you to lasting success!

APPENDIX A

Take Action!

Industrial real estate is a dynamic and ever-evolving field that requires continuous learning, observation, and networking to stay ahead. In this chapter, we'll explore actionable steps you can take to put your knowledge into practice and thrive in the industrial real estate market.

1. Start Reading and Stay Informed

To truly understand the industrial real estate market, you need to immerse yourself in the latest news, trends, and data. Start with the resources mentioned in chapter 34 but don't stop there. Constantly be on the hunt for new sources of information and perhaps most importantly – data!

Expert Insight

The real opportunity in industrial real estate is finding value where others don't—buying vacant buildings, improving their function, and turning them into cash-flowing assets. It's all about understanding the asset's function and being disciplined enough to stick to what you know.
—John Croft, President of Camrock Capital

2. Drive Through Industrial Parks

There's no substitute for getting out into the field and seeing industrial real estate firsthand.

Schedule time to:

- Observe Activity: Note the types of businesses, the condition of properties, and how tenants use their spaces.
- Identify Trends: Look for emerging developments, new construction, and vacancies.
- Understand the Layout: Driving through industrial parks will

give you a better sense of the flow of traffic, accessibility, and the presence of supporting infrastructure like railways or ports.

3. Build and Leverage Your Network

Success in industrial real estate often hinges on relationships. Take proactive steps to expand your network:

- Join Industry Groups: Organizations like NAIOP, SIOR, and CCIM offer valuable networking opportunities and educational events.
- Attend Local Events: Conferences, property tours, and real estate expos are great ways to meet industry professionals and stay updated on market trends.
- Collaborate: Reach out to brokers, appraisers, contractors, and other stakeholders for insights and potential partnerships.

4. Study the Local Market

Understanding your local market is crucial for making informed decisions. To deepen your knowledge:

- Analyze Comparable Properties: Look at recent sales and leases to gauge pricing trends and demand.
- Research Zoning and Regulations: Familiarize yourself with local zoning laws and their impact on industrial properties.
- Talk to Local Experts: Brokers, municipal planners, and property managers can provide invaluable insights into the market.

5. Utilize Technology and Tools

Take advantage of technology to enhance your decision-making:

- GIS Mapping Software: Use tools like CoStar or ESRI to visualize property data and market trends.
- Drone Footage: Aerial views can offer a better understanding of property layouts and surrounding infrastructure.
- Market Analytics Platforms: Subscription services like Real Capital Analytics (RCA) and LoopNet provide detailed property and market data.

6. Visit Properties and Ask Questions

Whenever possible, visit properties in person to:

- Assess Condition: Inspect the building's structure, roof, HVAC systems, and utilities.
- Evaluate Usability: Consider whether the property's layout, ceiling heights, and loading docks meet tenant requirements.
- Engage Owners or Managers: Ask about past tenants, property history, and maintenance records.

7. Do it!

Finally, it's not enough to simply gather information—you need to act on it. Some actionable steps include:

- Start Small: If you're new to the market, consider starting with a smaller investment to gain experience.
- Draft a Strategy: Develop a clear plan for how you'll approach industrial real estate, whether it's investing, leasing, or consulting.
- Track Your Progress: Regularly evaluate your successes and areas for improvement to refine your approach.

Expert Insight

"Start where you're comfortable, regardless of size or capital. Industrial real estate has shifted toward distribution recently, but with global supply chain challenges, manufacturing is coming back to North America. There's opportunity in both distribution and manufacturing—I'm optimistic about the market."
—Ryan Koehn, Managing Director of 18th Floor Developments

Key Takeaways

- Industrial real estate requires a mix of market knowledge, field experience, and strategic networking.
- Staying informed through market reports and industry news is essential for understanding trends and opportunities.
- Building a strong network and leveraging technology can give you a competitive edge.

- Actionable insights and hands-on research will set you apart as a knowledgeable and confident participant in the industrial real estate market.

By following these tips and continuously building on your expertise, you'll be well-equipped to navigate the complexities of industrial real estate and achieve your goals!

APPENDIX B

Further Reading

Behemoth: A History of the Factory and the Making of the Modern World by Joshua B. Freeman

Building the Modern World (Albert Kahn in Detroit) by Michael H. Hodges

Buildings for Industrial Storage and Distribution, 2nd Edition, Jolyon Drury and Peter Falconer

Cathedrals of Industry by Michael L. Horowitz and James P. Holtje

Commercial Building Construction: Materials and Methods by David A. Madsen

Commercial Property Analysis by Sauder School of Business Real Estate Division at UBC

Confessions of a Real Estate Entrepreneur by James Randel

Construction Management and Design of Industrial Concrete and Steel Structures by Mohamed A. El-Reedy

Creating Trinity: Blueprints of a Real Estate Entrepreneur & Investor by Gary Chesson

Educated REIT Investing: The Ultimate Guide to Understanding and Investing in Real Estate Investment Trusts by Stephanie Krewson-Kelly and Glenn R. Mueller

Essentials of Inventory Management, 2nd Edition by Max Muller

Factory Design by Chris Van Uffelen

Fagus: Industrial Culture From Werkbund to Bauhaus by Annemarie Jaeggi

Faster, Better, Cheaper in the History of Manufacturing: From the Stone Age to Lean Manufacturing and Beyond, by Christop Roser

Flow: How the Best Supply Chains Thrive by Rob Handfield and Tom Linton

Global Logistics and Supply Chain Management, 4th Edition, by John Mangan, Chandra Lalwani and Agustina Calatayud

How to Underwrite Industrial Commercial Real Estate by Ronald Rohde

Images of America: Bethlehem Steel by Tracy L. Berger-Carmen

Industrial Automation From Scratch, 1st Edition by Olushola Akande

Industrial Britain: An Architectural History by Huber Pragnell

Industrial Buildings in an Urban Context by Tongi University Press

Industrial Electricity, 10th Edition by Michael E. Brumbach

Industrial Heritage Re-tooled: The TICCIH Guide to Industrial Heritage Conservation (2012)

Industrial Heritage Sites in Transformation by Rotledge Studies in Herirage (2015)

Industrial Intelligence: The Executive's Guide for Making Informed Commercial Real Estate Decisions by Justin Smith

Industrial Mega Projects: Concepts, Strategies, and Practices for Success by Edward W. Merrow.

Industrial Real Estate by the Society of Industrial Realtors (1967)

Industrial Real Estate Investing and Management, by Obie Silverwood

Industrial Ventilation Design Guidebook: Volume 1 ,2nd Edition

Industry, Architecture and Engineering: American Ingenuity by Louis Bergeron and Maria Teresa Maiullari-Pontius

Infrastructure: A Guide to the Industrial Landscape, Revised and Updated Edition by Brian Hayes

Investing in Industrial Real Estate, by Ron Rohde

Just-in-Time Real Estate: How Trends in Logistics Are Driving Industrial Development by the Urban Land Institute (2004)

Land by Simon Winchester

Manufacturing Facilities Design & Material Handling, 6th Edition by Matthew P. Stephens

Manufacturing Processes for Design Professionals by Rob Thompson

My Forty Years with Ford by Charles E. Sorensen

Proto-Industrial Architecture of the Veneto: In the Age of Palladio by the Centro Internazionale Di Studi Di Architettura Andrew Palladio

Real Estate Development: Pricinciples and Process, 5th Edition, by Urban Land Institiute

Real Estate Finance and Investments, by Peter Linneman

The 99% Invisible City: A Field Guide to the Hidden World of Everyday Design by Roman Marks

The Architecture of Industry: Changing Paradigms in Industrial Building and Planning by Mathew Aitchison

The Economics of Industrial Development by John Weiss

The Geography of Transport Systems, 3rd Edition, by Jean-Paul Rodrigue

The Industrial Revolution in World History, 4th Edition by Peter N. Stearns

The Industrial Revolutionaries: The Making of the Modern World by Gavin Weightman

The Time, Space & Cost Guide to Better Warehouse Design: A Hands-on Guide to Help You Improve the Design and Operations of Your Warehouse or Distribution Center, 2nd Edition by the Distribution Group

The Toyota Way: 14 Management Principles from the World's Greatest Manufacturer, 2nd Edition by Jeffrey K. Liker

The Way to Go: Moving by Sea, Land, and Air by Kate Ascher

Warehouse Management: The Definitive Guide to Improving Efficiency and Minimizing Costs in the Modern Warehouse, 4th Edition by Gwynne Richards

World-Class Warehouse and Material Handling, 2nd Edition Edward H. Frazelle

APPENDIX C

Industrial Real Estate Glossary

Abatement: Often referred to as free rent or early occupancy, occurring outside or within the lease term.

Additive Manufacturing: Creating objects by adding material layer by layer; commonly known as 3D printing.

Air Curtain: Device above a door restricting air movement to maintain indoor temperature.

Automation: Use of technology or robotics to perform tasks with minimal human intervention.

Base Rent: Minimum rent, subject to increases over lease term.

Base Year: Reference year for calculating tenant's share of operating expense increases.

Big Box Industrial: Large industrial buildings (typically over 100,000 sq ft) for storage, distribution, or manufacturing.

BOMA: Building Owners and Managers Association; standardizes commercial building measurements.

Brownfield: Previously developed land potentially contaminated, requiring remediation.

Built-Up Roof (BUR): Roofing with alternating layers of tar and gravel.

Build-to-Suit: Facility constructed specifically to meet a tenant's operational needs.

Building Classifications: Categories (A, B, C) reflecting age, quality, and location of buildings.

Building Code: Municipal regulations dictating property use, design, materials, and safety.

Butler Building: A pre-engineered metal building system known for its modular design and quick assembly, commonly used in industrial and warehouse structures.

CCIM: Certified Commercial Investment Member; designation in commercial real estate.

Ceiling Height: Height from floor to roof of a building.

Class B Industrial: Industrial properties typically characterized by slightly older age, moderate construction quality, and less prominent locations compared to Class A properties. They often have lower clear heights, fewer loading options, and may require some upgrades or renovations. While not considered prime assets, Class B industrial facilities offer functional and cost-effective options appealing to a wide range of tenants looking for practical space in accessible, though secondary, locations.

Clear Ceiling Height: Usable vertical height from floor to lowest structural element.

Clear Span Roof: A roof structure designed without intermediate columns or structural supports, allowing for unobstructed open space beneath. This design maximizes usable interior area, offering significant flexibility for tenants who require large, open spaces for operations such as warehousing, distribution, or manufacturing processes.

Cold Storage: Temperature-controlled facilities for refrigerated or frozen goods.

Column Grid: Spacing arrangement of structural columns within a building affecting usable space and flexibility.

Contractor Garages: Industrial or flex properties specifically designed for tradespeople and contractors, typically featuring smaller individual units with drive-in access, overhead doors, storage areas for tools, equipment, or materials, and occasionally limited office space. These facilities cater to tenants such as plumbers, electricians, landscapers, and other trades, providing functional space suitable for operations and secure storage.

Cross Docking: Direct transfer of goods from incoming to outgoing trucks with minimal storage.

Distribution Center: Facility for receiving, storing, and distributing goods.

Dock-High Loading: Loading docks positioned at standard truck-bed height (approximately 48 inches).

Dock Leveller: Platform bridging gap between loading dock and truck.

Drive-In Racking: Storage allowing forklift access into racks for pallets.

E-Commerce: Online buying/selling of goods, boosting industrial real estate demand.

Easement: Legal right allowing use of someone else's property for specific purposes.

EIFS (Exterior Insulation and Finish System): A type of exterior building cladding that provides insulation and decorative finish in one integrated system, commonly applied to commercial buildings and warehouses.

Environmental Site Assessment (ESA): Study identifying environmental contamination risks.

ESFR (Early Suppression, Fast Response): Sprinklers quickly suppressing fires in high-piled storage.

Fire Rating: Classification indicating the duration a building component withstands fire.

Flex Industrial: Properties combining office, warehouse, and light manufacturing uses.

Gantry Crane: Mobile crane used in open or semi-enclosed spaces.

Greenfield: Undeveloped land for new construction projects.

Geotechnical Report: A detailed document prepared by geotechnical engineers, outlining soil composition, rock characteristics, groundwater conditions, and stability analyses for a specific site. This report provides critical recommendations for foundation design, construction methods, and mitigation of potential site-related risks in industrial real estate development.

HVAC: Systems regulating indoor heating, ventilation, and air conditioning.
Heavy Industrial: Properties designed for heavy manufacturing or processes requiring robust infrastructure.

Industrial Outdoor Storage (IOS): Outdoor storage for equipment, vehicles, or materials.
Internet of Things (IoT): Connected devices communicating over the internet for monitoring/control.

Light Industrial: Facilities for assembly, storage, office work; lighter infrastructure needs.
Loading Dock Configuration: Arrangement, dimensions, and functionality of loading docks.

Make-Up Air: Ventilation replacing exhausted air to maintain indoor quality.
Marshalling Area: Space for trucks preparing for loading/unloading.
Mezzanine: Intermediate floor within a warehouse maximizing vertical space.
Modified Bitumen Roofing: Asphalt-polymer roofing for enhanced waterproofing.

NAIOP: Commercial Real Estate Development Association.
Net Lease: Tenant covers some or all property expenses (taxes, insurance, maintenance).

Obsolescence (Building): Condition where a building becomes outdated or less functional.

Parking Ratio: A measure indicating the number of parking spaces provided per unit of building area, typically expressed per 1,000 square feet. Important for zoning compliance and tenant requirements.
Phase I ESA: Environmental report assessing contamination risks through historical records and inspection.
Phase II ESA: A detailed investigation conducted when a Phase I ESA identifies potential environmental contamination, involving soil, groundwater, and building material sampling to determine the presence and extent of pollutants.
Power: Electrical energy usage or production rate, measured in watts (W).
Precast Concrete: Concrete components manufactured off-site and assembled on-site.
Property Condition Report (PCR): Assesses property's physical condition and maintenance needs.

Rack Storage: Warehouse shelving for vertical/horizontal storage.
Rail Served/Access: A property or site with direct connectivity to rail infrastructure,

allowing goods to be loaded and unloaded directly from rail cars, highly desirable in logistics, manufacturing, and distribution operations.

REC (Recognized Environmental Condition): A term used in environmental site assessments (especially Phase I ESAs) to indicate the presence or likely presence of hazardous substances or petroleum products in, on, or at a property. An REC suggests a potential contamination issue that may require further investigation or remediation. This designation can impact financing, development plans, and liability concerns for industrial real estate properties.

Recessed Dock: A loading dock configuration in which the dock doors are set back into the building, creating an exterior staging or maneuvering area protected from weather and improving truck alignment. This design enhances loading efficiency, safety, and protects goods during the transfer process.

Retention Pond: Basin managing stormwater runoff.

Roof Load: Maximum weight a roof structure supports.

SIOR: Society of Industrial and Office Realtors; professional organization for industrial/office brokers.

Single-Ply Membrane: Synthetic roofing materials (TPO, PVC, EPDM).

Site Coverage Ratio (SCR): Land percentage covered by structures.

Small Bay Industrial: Industrial properties characterized by smaller, individually leased units typically ranging from 1,000 to 10,000 square feet. Often configured for multiple tenants, these spaces are suited for local businesses requiring flexible warehouse, showroom, office, or light manufacturing areas with convenient loading access.

Speed Bay: A designated loading and staging area in a warehouse or distribution facility, typically located adjacent to loading docks, designed to facilitate rapid movement, sorting, and transfer of goods. Speed bays enhance operational efficiency by reducing congestion and improving workflow between receiving, storage, and shipping areas.

Sump Drain: Collects and removes water from building/property low points.

TEU (Twenty-Foot Equivalent Unit): Standard cargo measures equal to a 20-foot container.

Tenant Improvements (TI): Modifications for specific tenant needs.

Tilt-Up Construction: Concrete panels cast on-site and tilted into place.

Trench Drain: Linear drain system for water management in industrial spaces.

Triple-Net Lease (NNN): Lease where tenant pays all property operating expenses.

Truck Court: Area for truck maneuvering, loading, unloading around warehouses.

Turn Radius: The minimum clear space required for vehicles, particularly trucks, to safely maneuver or turn without obstructions on a property, essential for industrial facility planning and site design.

Under Hook Height: Vertical lifting capacity determined by crane hook height.

Utilities: Essential services (electricity, water, gas, telecommunications).

Value-Add Investment: Investment requiring improvements to increase market value or rental income.

Warehouse: Facility for storing, distributing, or producing goods.
Warehouse Management System (WMS): Software optimizing inventory storage and retrieval.
Wet Pipe Sprinkler System: Fire suppression system with water-filled pipes for immediate response.

Yard Area: Outdoor space surrounding industrial facilities for storage or truck circulation.

Zoning: Regulations determining property use (industrial, commercial, residential).
Zoning Ordinance: Local statute controlling land use and improvements within specific zones.

Index of Figures

Index

www.ingramcontent.com/pod-product-compliance
Lightning Source LLC
Chambersburg PA
CBHW071856090426
42811CB00004B/632